CW00666204

The Ultimate Guide to
Surviving Your
Primary PGCE:
From Application to
Certification

By Rachael Gay

Copyright © 2019 by Rachael Gay

All rights reserved. No part of this book may be reproduced or used in any manner without written permission of the copyright owner except for the use of quotations in a book review. For more information, address: info@survivingyourpgce.com

FIRST EDITION

www.survivingyourpgce.com

About the Author

Rachael Gay has recently completed her Primary PGCE at Goldsmith's University in London. She decided to write her blog survivingyourpgce.com to help potential PGCE students prepare for the demands of the course.

CONTENTS

1
Introduction

'Let us remember: One book, one pen, one child, and one teacher can change the world.'

Malala Yousafzai

Well Done!

First of all, I would like to say well done!

You may be picking up this book after finding out you've been accepted on to a PGCE course or you may just be thinking about applying. It doesn't matter; you still deserve some praise.

Teaching is an incredibly stressful and demanding job and depending on who you speak to, everyone has differing opinions on how the PGCE year affected them. However, it is incredibly rewarding working with and shaping young minds as an educational professional.

So, once again, well done for choosing such a demanding but rewarding career.

Your PGCE Year

Your PGCE might just turn out the be the hardest thing you have ever done:

- You will spend some time at university. Depending on your personality, you may find this helpful or you may find it tedious. Either way, when you are on a placement, you might just find yourself longing for the 9am starts and undisturbed hour-long lunches.

- You will have several placements during the eight to nine months and some may not be close to home so expect early starts.

- Balancing both teaching and academic work will test your organisational skills.

- It will be very fast-paced. It won't feel like it sometimes, but it will pass in a flash.

Some days you will come home and feel like quitting after a bad observation. You will tell yourself teaching is just not for you. You will then go in the next day, deflated and feeling very sorry for yourself. In these moments, you will feel like you are the worst teacher to have ever stepped into your class.

And then something will shine some perspective on the situation. You will remember that during that 'bad' observed lesson, one of the children who has been struggling with adding three-digit numbers together finally understood what you've been teaching for the last two weeks. Another child, who has barely said two words to you since you arrived, told you about their evening at the park. One of the SEN children in your class was finally able to answer a question without extra support. In teaching, you must have perspective and try to look for the positives.

I will admit it can be hard to think of the positives when you have spent hours planning an exciting and engaging lesson for your class, only for a few to shout out how bored they are and then refuse to participate. This will nearly always be when you are being observed or in the middle of some sort of crisis and could really do without the added frustration.

But at the end of the day, you must remember one thing: they are just kids.

Children are not as good as adults at handling their emotions or knowing when their input is not required. They don't hate you and you are not an awful person. Like adults, they have their good and bad days. Unfortunately, they haven't yet developed a way of coping with the bad days quite as well.

Teaching is such a rollercoaster ride. I have had times where I have gone from wanting to cry to jumping for joy in just one lesson. For all the frustration, nothing will ever beat that feeling when a child has a 'lightbulb moment' and they finally understand something you have taught them. Being able to make a difference, even on such a small scale, daily, is just an amazing feeling.

Keeping All the Plates Spinning (Dealing with Life Outside of Your PGCE)

While the PGCE course only lasts a year, it will be a year that will not only test you but also your friends and family. Building a strong network around you will make the time so much more manageable.

Looking After Number One

I can't stress this enough: you need to look after yourself! Eating junk food, not getting much sleep and being in a constant state of stress is a recipe for disaster. The PGCE has a high dropout rate; as high as 33-40% according to The Guardian and the BBC. So, it is important to find ways of managing to cope.

- Bulk cook meals. Foods like lasagne, shepherd's pie and stews freeze really well. Go buy some of those plastic takeaway containers and spend some time making healthy and filling meals. One the days when you are starving but too tired to cook, all you have to do is defrost and then microwave them for a quick dinner. It also works out cheaper too!

- Find and maintain a hobby. Whether it's baking cakes or knitting scarves, you need to make sure you find something to do to de-stress from work. Ideally, you will find something that involves other people to help maintain perspective and to socialise with people.

- De-stressing routines. For some people, that might be going to the gym; for others, it might be binge-watching Netflix. My favourite way to wind down is to soak in a bubble bath with a novel. It doesn't really matter what you do as long as it relaxes you.

- Don't reinvent the wheel. This was one of the first things we were told during the PGCE. When planning a lesson, always have a look to see if someone else has planned something similar. You will need to adapt it to suit the needs of your class but it is so much easier to have a starting point. Later on in this book, I will show you where you can find some decent planning websites.

- Have faith in your ability. You were accepted on to the course, so your provider obviously thinks you have potential. Always remember that you are still learning. Some people will forget that and expect you to act exactly like an experienced teacher. It won't happen straight away: you need to learn how to behave like an experienced teacher. It will sometimes feel like you have 101 things to improve but start with one of them and keeping working at it until you master it.

Family and Friends

Before you start the course, I would highly recommend sitting down with both your family and friends and warning them about how busy you will be.

- Accept that you might not be able to help out as much as you used to. That doesn't mean you don't have to do the washing up, but you will need to work out a compromise. It might be as simple as doing your household jobs at the weekend or doing the weekly food shop on the way back from work (or even better, online!) I made the initial mistake of expecting other people to pick up the slack when I was busy. Trust me, this will put a strain on your relationship so don't do it.

- Depending on how willing your friends and family are, rope them in to help you with tasks. I managed to convince one friend to spend four hours laminating and cutting with me. Offering food or drink usually makes the idea more palatable.

- Try and make friends on your course. If you are very social, this won't be a problem but if you aren't, I would suggest trying. While there are plenty of forums you can ask advice from, nothing beats having a moan to a group of people who are going through the same thing as you. That being said, don't neglect your non-teaching friends as it is also important to be able to distance yourself from an educational environment and talk about non-teaching things.

A Note on Moving Away for Your Course

I wanted to add this part to the book as I don't think it got mentioned very much when I was looking for advice in regard to training. I decided to move over 150 miles away to do my course and, while the course offered what I wanted, it was very difficult being that far away from the people I cared about. I didn't go away for my initial degree, so this was my first time away to study. The decision about where to study will ultimately come down to personality and if you are a homebody or don't mind being away.

The pros

*   My partner was in university while I was away which meant we didn't see that much of each other as we were busy. This had the side effect of both of us spending a lot of free time on our work. So, when we did see each other, neither of us were stressed and we got to enjoy each other's company without all the normal petty arguments that come from stress.
*   Fewer arguments. As you are not around each other all the time, you can't argue as much.
*   You'll meet lots of new people.
*   You'll get to explore a new place.
*   You will learn a lot about yourself and what you can cope with.

The cons

*   When you do argue, arguments can go on for longer as you can just ignore the other person. Once, when I was very stressed, I didn't speak to my partner for six weeks over some silly disagreement.
*   It is hard living on your own if you haven't before. When you live with family or friends, you have someone who can do the washing up when you are too busy; on your own, it will just stay piled up. You'll need to work out a list of things you will do around the house (and when) and stick to it.
*   Money. You will have to support yourself while doing your course. You will struggle to maintain a job and, to be honest, I wouldn't recommend it.
*   You may feel isolated if you don't end up making friends.

2
Application

"The beginning is always today."

Mary Wollstonecraft Shelley

Eligibility

Despite all the nations being part of the United Kingdom, England, Northern Ireland, Scotland and Wales all have slightly different minimum entry requirements. While I am not an expert, I have included the following criteria as a guideline for the 2017-2018 academic year. I would strongly recommend checking with the universities you hope to attend as requirements may vary.

England

- An undergraduate degree (or equivalent)
- Grade C/4 in English Language and mathematics
- Grade C/4 in science if studying for a Primary PGCE
- Pass for both literacy and numeracy Professional Skills tests.

Northern Ireland

- An undergraduate degree (or equivalent)
- Grade C/4 in English Language and mathematics
- Grade C/4 in science if studying for a Primary PGCE

Scotland

- An undergraduate degree (or equivalent)
- SCQF Level 6 or above in English Higher Grade (or equivalent)
- SCQF Level 5 or above in mathematics (or equivalent)

Wales

- An undergraduate degree (or equivalent)
- Grade B in English Language and mathematics
- Grade C in Science if studying for a Primary PGCE

Notes on Eligibility:

- Please remember that these are the minimum entry requirements for a PGCE. Competition for PGCE places is fierce so anything extra you can add to your application would be advantageous.

- Most (if not all) providers will expect you to have completed some form of work experience in a primary school setting. This can vary between five and ten days depending on the university. I would highly recommend completing more than the minimum expected amount if you want your application to stand out. Experience in several different age ranges will strengthen your application as you will be able to justify why you have decided to apply for a particular age range.

Funding

It may seem like I am jumping the gun a little by writing about funding so soon into the application process, but it is important. Living on a Student Loan income is not going to work for everyone. The examples below are based on a range of different criteria. There are calculators you can use to tailor the amount of finance you will get; I have included details of these in each section.

Assumptions (2018-2019)		Living at Home with Parents	Living Away from Home Outside London	Living Away from Home Inside London
• Studying full time. • £9000 tuition fees • Household income is £30,000	England	• Tuition fee loan: up to £9250 • Maintenance loan: £7324	• Tuition fee loan: up to £9250 • Maintenance loan: £8700	• Tuition fee loan: up to £9250 • Maintenance loan £11,354
	Northern Ireland	• Tuition fee loan: up to £9250 • Maintenance loan: £3750 • Grant: up to £ 3475	• Tuition fee loan: up to £9250 • Maintenance loan: £4840 • Grant: up to £ 3475	• Tuition fee loan: up to £9250. • Maintenance loan: £6780 • Grant: up to £ 3475
	Scotland	• Tuition fee loan: £1820 if studying in Scotland and up to £9250 if outside • Maintenance loan: £5750 • Bursary: £500	• Tuition fee loan: £1820 if studying in Scotland and up to £9250 if outside • Maintenance loan: £5750 • Bursary: £500	• Tuition fee loan: £1820 if studying in Scotland and up to £9250 if outside • Maintenance loan: £5750 • Bursary: £500

	Wales	• Tuition fee loan: up to £9250	• Tuition fee loan: up to £9250	• Tuition fee loan: Up to £9250
		• Maintenance loan: £5930	• Maintenance loan: £6947	• Maintenance loan: £8643
		• Grant: £1720	• Grant: £2053	• Grant: £2607

These are just guidelines for what you can expect. Each country will have its own way of calculating entitlement. It would also be beneficial to have a look at the relevant Student Finance website as there may also be extra grants for students from low-income households, or for things like travel costs.

- England calculator: https://www.gov.uk/student-finance-calculator

- Northern Ireland calculator: http://www.studentfinanceni.co.uk/portal/page?_pageid=54,1266217&_dad=portal&_schema=PORTAL

- Scotland calculator: http://www.saas.gov.uk/full_time/ug/young/funding_available.htm

- Wales calculator: https://www.studentfinancewales.co.uk/calculator.aspx#.WhLF8bacZAY

Helpful Tip

- If you still really want to teach but finances are worrying you, you may be eligible for a paid School Direct course. You are paid a salary and it is mostly school-based. It can be challenging to gain a place on this course, but it may be an option for some trainee teachers. More information can be found here: https://www.gov.uk/guidance/funding-initial-teacher-training-itt-academic-year-2017-to-18

- If you have a degree in a 'shortage subject' (mathematics, biology, physics, chemistry, computing, languages and geography) and are willing to train in this area, you could gain some extra financial help in the form of a bursary. These do not have to be paid back. Examples can be found here: https://getintoteaching.education.gov.uk/funding-and-salary/overview

- Do check universities' own websites too. Some will have their own grants available for you to apply for.
- Turn2us is a brilliant website to use to search for extra grants. Here is the link: https://grants-search.turn2us.org.uk

Choosing a University

If you are reading this book then you will be familiar with this situation; it is the same as when you were choosing a university for your undergraduate degree. However, while you can apply most of the same principles you used for your degree, such as location and good reviews, there are other things to consider.

Location:

Does the university have good transport links? If you are staying on campus, does it have a good range of local amenities? Universities will put a limit on how far you will be expected to travel to a placement from your home. An hour limit in London will be a very different travelling experience to an hour from Swansea!

Course Layout:

Will you do blocks of time in university? Or will you go to university on 'day release'? Does the university offer subject specialisms? Will you have many smaller 1000-word essays or two larger 5000-word dissertations?

Teaching Ethos of the University:

Does the university encourage you to be creative and experiment? Is it a university that relies heavily on research and expects the same of you? Does the university seem laid-back or strict? Does the university have a high ranking?

Some of these questions may only be answered at interview, but it is worth sitting down and having a think about things which are important to you. This is a very personal decision and what would appeal to your parents or friends may not appeal to you. You should listen to others' opinions as they may have thought of something you haven't but, at the end of the day, it is you taking the course and not them. This research will pay off when you come to write your personal statement as you will want to include information that appeals to the university you are applying for. For example, there would be no point in showcasing how creative you are if the university does not seem to consider that a priority when choosing a potential student.

Finding Information

I urge you to do as much research as you can before you apply to a university. Thankfully, there are plenty of places to look for advice:

- The university website
- Brochures
- Student Room forum
- Attend open days
- The Complete University Guide
- Talk to people who have been to the university
- PGCE student blogs

I would advise that you check a few sources rather than relying on just one. While blogs and posts on forums may not offer statistical information, it offers you the chance to see what gripes students have about the university and if these would irritate you too. Take some of these reviews with a pinch of salt as some people will always find something to moan about.

Open Days:

One thing I would highly recommend is visiting the university on one of their open days. Not only can you see the potential campus and ask questions, but you also have something to talk about when you go to an interview. Do make sure you attend the housing tours if you require housing while on the course. There is no point in applying to a university where the housing is a long bus ride away or has very poor reviews if either of those things would put you off.

One Last Tip:

In the unlikely event that you are not offered a place at any of your three university choices, I would always recommend having a backup fourth choice. Do the same research as you would for your first three choices. This will save time should you need to use Apply 2.

Experience

With PGCE courses typically oversubscribed, it is essential that you gain some form of experience prior to even applying for a place on a course. There are several reasons why this is important:

- You need to know that working for children is for you. We have all seen films featuring inspirational teachers (Dead Poets Society, I am looking at you!) The children make huge leaps in progress and there aren't thirty children screaming for attention. But that is not reality. Children are amazing to work with, but they are demanding. Gaining experience will help you to tell if you really want to work with them.

- During your interview, you may be asked a question about your experience and the impact it has had on you. You will appear far more appealing to a prospective university if you can answer an interview question with an example of something that happened during a work experience placement.

- It is a sad fact to acknowledge but teachers are leaving the profession in high numbers. Search the internet and you will find many teachers saying something along the lines of, 'I wish I knew how hard it was going to be'. While you can't predict how hard your teaching career will be, it is important to gain as much experience as possible, so you can at least walk into a career with some idea of both the positive and negative aspects.

How Much Experience Should I Gain?

How long is a piece of string? No university is going to decline you for having too much experience. The more experience you have, the more attractive you are as a candidate as providers can see that you are unlikely to leave during the course (and cost them funding) because you know what you want.

Before applying for a PGCE, I gained the following experience:

- I worked for two years as an Activity Leader during my Summer and Easter break. This involved taking children on tours and planning evening activities for them.

- I completed a university experience passport. As part of the certificate, I had to gain 70 hours experience in a primary school.

- I took a TESOL course as part of my degree. In addition to now being able to teach English abroad, it also gave me brilliant skills for my PGCE, such as lesson planning.

- I taught for a few weeks in the last summer of my undergraduate degree. I had passed my TESOL course so was qualified. Although I taught mostly teenagers, similar principles about planning and engagement can be applied to all year groups.

- I had experience as a Teaching Assistant with an agency.

This may seem a lot but over a four-year period (I took a year out after my degree) it isn't very much. If you decide to take a year out, one piece of advice I would offer is to complete a Teacher Assistant Level Two or Three qualification. I completed mine online with DCA Home Learning but there are plenty to choose from. I was able to complete it quickly and had to do tests at home on the computer after I had studied a few chapters. Once you have a qualification, you may be required by an agency or school to complete a few days of work experience before they will employ you. Being qualified allows you to earn some money while you gain valuable experience for a PGCE. It's a win-win scenario.

A Note on Online Courses:

Before you choose a course, make sure it is from a reputable company and accredited with a recognised exam board. I was lucky with DCA as my partner had used them and gained jobs with the qualification, so I knew they were legitimate. Ask friends and family if they could recommend an online course provider that they have used or, alternatively, ask your university as they may be able to recommend someone. Failing that, online reviews are very useful in determining whether a company is trustworthy.

Try to gain experience in different age ranges, not just the range you would like to work in. As part of my course, we had to gain experience in both the key stage below and above the one we specialised in. It will be a lot less daunting going from a Year Three class to a Year Nine class for the day if you have already worked with secondary school children.

Ways to Gain Experience:

- Do you have days off during the week while at university? Arrange to spend one day a week at a school. You will become familiar to the school and, if you like it there, you could even arrange to do one of your placements there during your course. If you did one day a week in a school over the course of your degree, you would gain one hundred and seventeen days of experience.

- Does your local area have any sports clubs or other out of school events? While time in a school is desirable, it looks really good on an application to show that you have interests outside of school that could be used by any future employer. It also helps prove you have teamwork skills.

- Do you have a Teaching Assistant qualification? You could gain some paid work through an agency.

- Do you play a musical instrument or have a degree in a primary school curriculum subject? You could advertise as a tutor. It will give you valuable experience of teaching children how to do something in a one-to-one setting.

If you are going to work with children, it will be expected that you have a valid DBS certificate. When I completed work experience in a local school (unpaid) for the first time, the local council paid for my DBS. Later, when I worked with an agency, I paid through them.

In the appendix, I have included a draft of a letter that could be sent to a school you would like to gain work experience in. This can also be found on the website.

Personal Statements

If you have only recently completed your undergraduate degree, you will be familiar with the idea of a personal statement. For those of you who don't know what a personal statement is, it is a small essay of around 1000 words where you have the chance to sell yourself and show off a bit. I know it can be daunting to write so much about yourself but now is not the time to be modest. You will be up against plenty of other students who will well-versed in this skill so you need to stand out.

Of course, you must not lie on your application. If you didn't run an intervention group for underprivileged children then don't put in your statement. If, however, you helped your class teacher run a reading group during your work experience placement then, of course, put that in.

I was once given some very good advice from a college tutor: show, don't tell. Instead of saying:

'I am good at working in teams/ I am a team player,'

you should instead 'show' that you are a team player by giving an example:

'I possess good teamwork skills which I honed when running an after-school football club with three other coaches. As part of my role, I had to liaise with all three coaches to find out their availability which I could then share with children's parents.'

Sounds better, right? I haven't exaggerated or made it sound forced. I have just given an example so the reader can see proof of my ability. Being able to give examples like this will help enormously in teaching interviews .

Putting Pen to Paper

Most people won't be able to write their statement in one go without preparation. That is why, with a quick look on Google, you will find hundreds of websites offering help with planning your statement. The best place to start would be UCAS:

https://www.ucas.com/ucas/teacher-training/apply-and-track/
how-write-ucas-teacher-training-personal-statement

UCAS have included some helpful tips on how to write your statement and what to include. Another good source of information is The Student Room. If you are having particular trouble wording something, it can be a good place to ask advice. Most universities also offer graduate support, so you may also be able to ask your university Careers Office for help.

Okay, so let's start. I have included a skeleton plan in the appendix to help you jot down some ideas for what to include in your statement. The following points below are also designed to get you think about what you may want to include. .

Step One: Why did you want to become a teacher? Did you have a brilliant teacher who inspired you? Do you want to make a difference? One of the reasons I wanted to be a teacher is because I didn't have a great experience in school when it came to subjects like mathematics. I was advised not to list 'poor teaching' as the reason why I wanted to teach. Instead, I made it into a positive. I mentioned that I struggled and felt stupid because I didn't understand maths, and I didn't want another child to feel like that; one of my motivations was to be able to help children who may be struggling to be able to access the curriculum.

Step Two: Do you understand the rewards and challenges of working with children? How can you prove this? You can mention (briefly) specific times where you have dealt with challenging children and how you resolved the situation. In my work experience placement, I had one child who refused to work during maths. I was worried I would look like I couldn't cope so would try and persuade the child to work by saying that they would lose their break if they didn't complete a certain amount. I even offered a reward of a break when they finished. Nothing was working. It was only after some research into the ways children can react if they feel they can't do something that I found this child was actually unconfident in maths and so reacting the way he was. So, I changed tactics and instead asked him how he was finding the work. Did he understand it? Could he explain it to me as I am not very good at maths? He did attempt to explain but obviously didn't understand. Rather than say that, I instead acted like he was right.

'Ah, I see,' I said. 'I have to see how many times I can put three into fifteen, not add them together. Let me have a go then to see if I understand.' I modelled what I had to do. Of course, he agreed I was right, but he thought he had explained it to me. Some children respond to this approach as it is less stressful than having to re-explain all the time. This shows both the challenges and the rewards of teaching in one example. If you wanted to include an example like this one, I would recommend slimming it down to avoid eating into your word count.

Step Three: Gather all paperwork. Did you do any courses outside of school like a Teaching Assistant course? How has your education benefitted you? Show how you are passionate about education.

Step Four: Think about your extra work experience. Did you run a club for your work experience? Maybe you did some tutoring? How have these prepared you for teaching?

Step Five: Do you have any extra skills? Do you play an instrument? Do you enjoy making creative items in your spare time? How about a passion for reading? How could these be useful in a teaching career?

Once you have got these basic ideas in note form, you have the start of your personal statement. If you are worried about how to start, I would suggest looking at some examples. I always found the beginning was the hardest so left that until last. As long as the finished statement is coherent, it doesn't matter which order you start in.

Once you have finished, get someone with good proofreading skills to go over your statement to check for any errors. They might also be able to offer something extra to add to your statement too.

Passion is also an important thing to showcase on your statement. Think: why am I passionate about education and becoming a teacher? You can have all the experience in the world and have worked in the best schools but if you can't convince someone you are passionate about teaching then maybe you need to have a think about why you want to be a teacher (as opposed to an accountant, for example).

Two Very Important Points:

- Check the word count before you start. It may change but currently it is 4000 characters or 47 lines of writing. You will be entering this into the UCAS system so there may be slight differences compared to your word processor. It is fine to be under the word count as long as you have included everything you need to.

- DO NOT, I REPEAT, DO NOT, COPY ANYONE ELSE'S STATEMENT! UCAS has software that can detect if you have copied another person's statement. There is nothing wrong with seeking inspiration or even tweaking a generic sentence, but you must not copy and paste someone else's work. Your application will immediately be rejected. It just isn't worth it.

References

Here is a tip I was given when applying for my first degree:

Ask your referees if you can use them and let them know when to expect your reference request.

While at college, I can remember reading on student forums about several students whose applications were delayed due to a late reference. My own PGCE application was delayed by a few days while I was waiting for a referee to submit my reference.

As with everything to do with the PGCE, time is of the essence. There are scaremongers who will convince you that if you don't have your application done the minute the system opens you will fail to gain a place. While this isn't strictly true, I have laid out this chapter to ensure you have everything ready to complete your application as quickly as possible. It is important to note that your application cannot be processed unless all parts of the application are completed. PGCE spaces go quickly; by having everything ready to go, I was able to send my application off within days.

Filling Out a Reference Request

The process for filling out the application is fairly simple.

You will need for each person:

- Their title
- First and second name
- Email
- Occupation
- Address (use their work address)
- Telephone/fax number

You will have to do this for two referees: a principal and secondary.

- Principal referee: Someone from your university if you graduated within the last five years, or an employer if it has been longer.
- Secondary referee: Someone who can comment on your character. An employer or someone you have completed

work experience with is acceptable.

Once you have completed and saved the information for both referees, you can ask for reference requests to be sent. The referee will be sent an online form to fill in which will be linked to your account. The reference form is not very long but the referee will need to write a statement about your character and ability. They have up to 47 lines to do this, although they don't have to use up all of this allowance. This can be time-consuming and not something you want to be rushed. This is why it is important to give as much notice as possible before asking someone to complete this form.

If your reference is unsure what to include, you can guide them to this website for guidance:

https://www.ucas.com/advisers/references/
how-write-ucas-teacher-training-references

Your referee can also see your application so will be able to gain some information from it. You, however, will be unable to see what your referee has written.

Note-

As your referee can see your application, I would advise you to refrain from fabricating information. By all means, show off your achievements, but your referees can report false information.

More information can be found here about references:

https://www.ucas.com/ucas/teacher-training/apply-and-track/
references-ucas-teacher-training-applications

Application Through UCAS

The aim of this chapter is to help you fill in your application. There is quite a lot to get through but don't worry, you can save your application and come back. If you have already compiled the information I mentioned in the previous sections, this should be a quick activity. The exact dates on which UCAS opens and closes vary so it is best to check their website regularly.

1. Register: You will need to fill in basic information like your name, address and date of birth. You will be given a username (your email) and will need to set a password. After this, you will receive an email containing a Personal ID which is required every time you log in to UCAS. Terms and Conditions will also need to be signed.

2. Other Personal Information: Nationality, resident status and disclosure of any disabilities or criminal convictions.

3. Additional Information (UK applications only): Your ethnicity and national identity.

4. University and Programme: You have up to three choices of university. You can also search for choices if you are still undecided. You do not have to use all three choices, but it is best to apply to more than one in case you don't get your preferred option.

5. Your Education: You need to list the qualifications that you have or will have before the PGCE course starts. This includes GCSEs, A-Levels and degree courses. You will also be asked to list your highest level of qualification; for most people, this will be their undergraduate degree. If you've passed your professional skills tests (England only) then you will also need to confirm this.

6. School and Work Experience: You need to add each placement individually. For each placement, you will need to include:

   a. Name of the school or place of work, job role, summary of experience and hours per week.

   b. For a PGCE, you only need to include relevant work experience or jobs. Some universities will require a full work history, but the individual university will let you know if they do. If you have space, feel free to include the jobs that aren't strictly relevant; if you can show transferable skills, such as working under pressure or to deadlines, then this can help your application.

7. Personal Statement: You can add your statement here. Check it fits the 4000 characters/47 line limit and edit your statement if it does not fit. It is better to be slightly under the word limit than slightly over and have to worry about editing at this late stage. Your statement should be applicable to all your university choices; try not to be too specific to any one university unless you are only applying to that particular institution.

8. References: You should have let your chosen referees know to expect an email from UCAS. Referees have two weeks to complete the application and will be sent a reminder if the two weeks pass without the reference being completed.

9. Pay the Fee: £24 if payable for your application once you have completed it. If you are unsuccessful in being accepted for any of your choices, you can apply again via APPLY 2 and will not be charged a second time.

Once everything has been submitted, your offers can be found through Track. Your application will automatically convert so you don't need to do anything.

Changes: You have seven days in which you can make amendments to your application, but you are only allowed to do this once.

When will you hear back?

Providers have up to 40 working days to reply to your application. If they do not reply, your application will be deemed unsuccessful.

Where can I check key dates?

This section of the UCAS website will help: https://www.ucas.com/ucas/events/find/scheme/teacher-training/type/key-date

Interviews

You've filled in your UCAS application and your referees have finally got back to you after your third email to them. You can finally breathe easily. That is until you get offered an interview at your first-choice university. Cue panic....

There is really no need to stress over these interviews. When I was preparing for my interviews I was struck with complete and overwhelming panic. What if I said the wrong thing? What if the tutor didn't like me? What if everyone else there knew more than me? What if I didn't get in? After spending what was probably an unhealthy amount of time googling interview techniques, I came across some advice:

Remember, you are also interviewing them. They are trying to impress you too.

Now, don't jump on a high horse and walk into your interview like you are some big shot. That's not what this advice is about. PGCE courses are extremely competitive (there are not many options) and also demanding (many people drop out). Tutors will be looking for:

A. Someone who is 100% passionate about becoming a teacher and who has done their research.
B. Someone who won't just quit when the going gets tough.
C. Someone who they feel is safe to work with children (I hope this goes without saying).

All you really have to do is make sure the person interviewing you can see you hit those three criteria. If you are a good candidate with the potential to be "outstanding" (good experience, passionate, proven record of sticking with things etc.) they know you will be applying to other courses and will be keen to have you; someone who needs a bit of polishing to become outstanding is a more attractive option than someone who needs to be taught everything from scratch. Tutors are also looking for someone who understands it's going to be a tough year but will finish the course. You also need to find a university where you feel you fit in and that understands the way you work.

When I left my interview, I knew immediately that I wanted to go to that university, even though it was actually my third choice. In hindsight, maybe I should have gone to my other interviews, but I followed my gut instinct. The university I eventually ended up in is well-known for being creative which is something I am passionate about. It also felt like you weren't just part of a sea of unknown faces; the tutors were approachable and seemed supportive. These few things meant a lot to me. I had already completed my research on different locations and the course, so I just had to make my mind up about what felt right.

So, during the interview process, don't be intimidated into not asking questions about how long the course runs or how assignments are assessed. At the end of the day, it is best you go into your PGCE knowing all of the facts rather than finding out later that the course is not quite right for you. The way I see it is this: if a tutor takes umbrage to you asking how many hours you will be in university each day (I did ask this) or any other reasonable question, then maybe it's not the university for you.

Structure of the Interview:

All interviews will vary slightly. Most universities will send you out some advice on how the day will be structured when they offer you an interview. If they don't, go online and have a look at The Student Room as there are normally a few threads from prospective students asking how to succeed in the interview.

My half day interview included:

- A timed mathematics assessment
- A timed written assessment
- A timed phonics assessment
- A discussion on an article I had been sent by the university
- A group task
- An interview with a tutor

The morning seemed to go very quickly and hadn't even reached home when I was called by the university to offer me a conditional place. I was glad I did some research into what to expect as I became more aware of what the tutors were looking for and I could then emphasise this during the morning.

What to Expect:

Below are a few tasks that may come up during your interview and an explanation of what you should do for each one. This is not a comprehensive list but the most common examples.

You are sent an article to read:

You will need to be able to discuss the points raised in this article. It would also be a good idea to read around this topic (TES is always very helpful for this) and be able to mention key ideas or theories. You don't need to be able to recite the article, but you will want to show that you have the initiative to research additional information about an unknown topic for discussion.

You are told there will be a discussion:

You will most likely be given an article or key area to research (safeguarding, for example). If you are not, it is a safe bet to research key issues that affect education. As in the previous example, you need to be able to discuss the topic and give your own view about it. During your interview, I would steer clear of anything too controversial (maybe don't say you think the reforms Michael Gove brought in were brilliant!)

You are told there will be tests:

As part of your teacher training, you will have to show development. The results of these tests will help you to make future targets towards this. Don't worry if you are not great at maths; these tests aren't necessarily used against you. Typically, they are used to see what support you will need.

- Maths: Brush up on addition, subtraction, multiplication and division. Also, conversion (fractions, decimals and percentages), money, basic algebra, geometry and word problems.

- Written English tasks: Spelling, punctuation, grammar, sentence structure and editing skills. Knowing grammatical terms will also help you ('A verb is a "doing word"' is what I was taught in school). If you have done a practical task, you may be asked to write about that or even, why you want to become a teacher.

- Phonics Test: Identify key terminology and segment words to find out how many sounds are in them.

You should have at least a B/C in both Mathematics and English Language already; as the tests are aimed at this level, you shouldn't have too much of a problem.

You are told there will be a presentation or you'll have to teach something:

First of all, don't panic!

The tutors are not expecting you to be able to teach like a qualified teacher. They are looking to see your potential. Some people don't cope well when they have to stand in front of a group of people and this will be off-putting to the children you want to teach. You will want to make a brief plan of what you intend to teach (starter, main and plenary) as well as an intention. You will also want to try and include any teaching methods that are currently in favour (such as talk partners).

Here is a very basic example:

- Learning Intention: Children will be able to recognise the three primary colours in French.
- Starter: (talk partners) discuss – can anyone name the three primary colours? (1 min)
- Main:
  - o Feedback (hands up and choose three people- a low ability, middle ability and high ability child, if known, to check understanding) (30 seconds)
  - o Flashcards – the teacher says the word, then the children repeat. Use silly voices such as 'baby', 'posh', 'monster' etc.) (2 mins)
- Plenary: Teams have to name the colour of the item. Show items such as an apple (red)

This sort of task can be adapted for all sorts of topics, such as teaching a new phonics sound.

Team Tasks

For my interview, I had to bring in a newspaper and we were told to make an item to help learning in the classroom. The other team made a microphone with empowering words on the side, whereas I suggested a model aqueduct for the team I was in. I had completed a similar task while working where we had to make a bridge. The beauty of the aqueduct was that it tied into the curriculum: geography (landscapes), history (the Romans) and science (water and gravity). This showed the tutors that I was aware of the curriculum and how I could take a cross-curricular approach to planning.

A Word on Behaviour at the Interview

I know this will seem like an odd subtitle that you may think you know the answer to already, so I apologise if it seems a bit like a rant. As I have mentioned before, the PGCE is highly competitive. This means that you cannot afford to carry other people through the interview process. Without sounding too ruthless, don't let other people take credit for your ideas; now is not the time to be modest. I am not saying you should walk up to a tutor and complain someone took your idea but, on the same token, make sure you don't just say nothing. Show you know what you are talking about. I have had this happen in lectures (where it doesn't really matter but is annoying) and I ended up not saying anything as I felt someone else had already mentioned my point. But when it happened again, I made sure I added to the original point with something that showed I knew what I was talking about. I am not saying throw anyone under the bus, but make sure people are not taking advantage. There are a lot of kind people in education and sometimes, in their effort to help, they get stepped on. If someone does say (for whatever reason) they haven't read an article, be kind and give them a quick summary. Just don't let it become a pattern.

I would also suggest making sure you don't come across as "bossy". I know, if you are anything like most teachers, you can't help taking charge- after all, that will soon be a large part of your job. However, resist the urge to take over and show instead that you can work as a team. You can learn a lot from your peers and hearing views that you won't always agree with will help you to develop your own views in education.

The Tutor Interviews

This can often seem the scariest bit. With discussions and group tasks, you are able to bounce ideas off other students. Now, it's all down to you. But just to set your mind at rest, the tutors are not trying to trick you. They don't expect you to know it all so don't try and pull the wool over their eyes and come across as a know-it-all. The tutors are people and being polite and showing enthusiasm will go a long way.

It is the role of the interviewer to determine if you would be a good fit on the course and to decide if they think you could cope with its demands. That is why it is so important to be honest about your experience and what you hope to gain from the PGCE.

Some good advice I would particularly like to share is to be prepared with scenarios and examples. Over the next few pages, I will provide some example questions and ways in which to answer them. If you can "show" with an example, rather than just using a textbook answer, you will come across as someone who understands the role of a teacher and is able to be self-critical. Even when things do not go as planned, being able to reflect on the problem and correct it next time is a valuable and often used skill in teaching.

Example Questions:

- **Why do you want to be a teacher?** Whatever you do, do not say anything about the number of holidays. That is the quickest way to wind up any teacher. What you do want to do is show that you have thought about teaching as a career and that it is not your "backup plan". I would also steer clear of using negative examples such as "I didn't have great teachers, so I want to be better than them." Again, the tutors won't take kindly to a member of their profession being judged by someone who hopes to join it. Instead, focus on the brilliant teachers you had. In my interview, I mentioned a secondary school history teacher who really made me enjoy the subject by using occasional sport or current affairs analogies. It made history seem more relevant. It is a harder question than it sounds, especially for people who have just always known they want to be a teacher. But you have to be able to explain this to a total stranger. If you are completely stuck, I would either ask current teachers why they entered the profession or go online and read examples other people have used. Don't copy them, but see if they have explained how you feel in a more succinct manner.

- **What are your strengths/ weaknesses?** Now is not the time to be modest. Ask friends, family and co-workers to help. Try and relate them to teaching, such as being highly organised or creative. When talking about weaknesses, put a positive spin on them. For example, if you are not the most organised person, explain to the tutor how you've bought a new planner, set up a new filing system for all your lecture notes and consistently get up ten minutes early to make sure you have all your work for the morning prepared. You are showing that you can reflect on something and then change it.

- **Can you give an example of when you used a positive behaviour management technique?** You may not be able to give many examples but show that you are aware of the term. Most educators will have come across a child that point-blank refuses to do what they are asked. What did you do in this situation? How did it turn out? If you really can't think of an example, you can mention someone else's practice and why it was good. Do not criticise their practice; it's about being reflective.

- **What experience do you have in primary education? Which age range is your favourite?** If you have got this far, you must have some experience of working in schools. Mention the age ranges you have experience in. You can also mention any clubs you have run, such as a youth club or sports team. If you do have a preferred age range, you'll be expected to elaborate on why that is the case. I like KS1 as I find their enthusiasm and sense of wonder a joy to teach. I also know teachers who would find KS1 children highly demanding and draining. It is a personal preference. As part of the PGCE, you will be expected to teach a variety of age ranges so don't get too stuck on only wanting to teach a certain age.

- **What qualities do you think a good teacher possesses?** Enthusiasm, reliance, subject knowledge, a sense of humour and empathy are all good examples. Whatever examples you use, make sure you can use them to relate to yourself- ideally, with examples.

- **Can you tell me a time when you dealt with a safeguarding issue?** Read the safeguarding document from a school in which you have recently gained experience. Most examples you give will have resulted in you passing on the information the child told you to the correct member of the safeguarding team.

- **What do equal opportunities mean to you in a classroom setting?** This question will most likely require an answer in regard to SEND children. How can you make sure everyone can access learning? Do you have experience in dealing with this issue? Have you seen a really good example?

- **What would your classroom look like?** The interviewer isn't just asking about what colour scheme you would use. Yes, mention you would have displays and a working wall for literacy and numeracy. But also mention the personal touches, such as having the children's work on display or inspirational quotes in the reading corner. You also want to mention the classroom atmosphere. During my training, I got into the habit of playing classical music during "long writes" (all the better if it matched the music to the theme of the work). The classroom was calmer and there was less chatting; I had control over the class without having to be draconian.

- **What current issues are we facing in education?** TES is a good place to start looking for current issues. Avoid going into great detail about anything too negative.

- **Can you recall a lesson you observed that you thought was good and why?** Again, don't be critical. Good examples include ingenious ways of teaching something; pace; clear learning intentions; and varied use of differentiation strategies.

These are just some examples. For more questions and extra support, try the Get into Teaching website:

https://getintoteaching.education.gov.uk/blog/
common-interview-questions

What to Do If You Get More Than One Interview?

Firstly, well done for getting more than one interview!

Before you go to an interview, it is best that you sit down and think about why you want to go to this particular university. Have a look at the location, costs, transport links, reviews on forums and the course layout. Before I went to any interviews, I had already decided which universities were my first, second and third choice. I ended up going with my third choice, purely as I liked the vibe I got from the staff and campus. This is not the best way to choose a university. As long as the interviews are on different days, I would suggest going to them all. Universities have 40 working days to either accept or reject your application. Once you have offers from all three institutions, you then have ten working days to make up your mind. If you have already rated the universities then, should you get an offer from them all, as long as you have a good feeling about the place, you would pick your first choice. This early groundwork will save a lot of time later on as you will have done all the research while waiting to be called to interview.

If you get offered two interviews on the same day then there are two things you can do:

1. Email your lower choice university and ask if it is possible to reschedule. Now, by doing this, you are letting that university know that they are your second option and they might not be willing to change the date.
2. Go to the university you feel is a better fit for you. This should be your first choice of university based on all the facts considered before.

What Should I Take?

Most universities will give you a list of things to take with you, but if in doubt:

*   A copy of your CV
*   Professional skills test results (if applicable)
*   Original copies of GCSE, A-Level and degree certificates
*   A passport picture with your name and date of birth on the back
*   ID (passport, driving license or NI card)

To save time, I would also make photocopies of the above and take them with you.

Professional Skills Tests

Before you are offered an unconditional place, you must have completed the professional skills tests in both literacy and numeracy.

Taking the tests:

- You will have to go to a Learn Direct Centre to take the tests on a computer. Some questions will be delivered audibly, and some will be written on the screen.
- You can only take the tests three times in two years. If you fail to pass the tests in this period, then you will be unable to take them again for two years.
- The first test is free. For each subsequent test, there is a £19.25 charge.

Numeracy Test:

- The test has 28 questions: 12 mental maths questions and 16 written questions.
- The test takes just under 50 minutes to complete.
- Key subjects to revise for the mental maths test:
  - o BIDMAS
  - o Fractions, decimals and percentages (and converting between the three)
  - o Time
  - o Proportion
  - o Measurement
  - o Conversion
- Key subjects to revise for the written maths test:
  - o Data handling
  - o Several step word problems
- You will be given paper or a whiteboard to help you work out your answers. There is also an onscreen calculator for parts of the test.

Literacy Test:

- The test lasts 45 minutes.
- The test is broken down into sections:
  - o Spelling test: words you will most likely use in a professional capacity (10 marks)
  - o Punctuation: adding the correct punctuation to a text (15 marks)
  - o Grammar: how to apply grammar, not just the grammatical terms (10-12 marks)
  - o Comprehension: making deductions, fact vs opinion and identifying pieces of information (10-12 marks)
- The test is not assessing your understanding of the National Curriculum.

Booking Your Tests:

- You can take your test anywhere that has a Learn Direct Centre.
- Busy centres may have long wait times so book early.
- At the test centre, you will need two forms of ID.
- You will also need evidence of a PGCE application. Your UCAS welcome letter or a print out of your application may be accepted. Always call ahead to check what the centre would prefer.
- Make sure you bring everything you need as, if you do not and you are not allowed to sit the test, it will still count towards one of your three attempts.

Pass Mark:

Each test varies on the pass mark. Harder tests will have a lower pass threshold and easier tests will have a higher threshold. All tests will be slightly different and so the difficulty levels will vary. The official pass mark is currently 63%.

As soon as you finish your test, you will be given a paper copy of your results. Within 48 hours, you should be able to access the online version. You will need to amend your UCAS application to show that you have passed. You have three years from the date of passing to use the tests towards a teaching application. After this point, you will need to re-sit them.

Re-sits:

*   You will have to pay £19.25 for every re-sit.
*   You have to wait at least 48 hours from sitting your last test before you can reapply.
*   It is best to give yourself a few more weeks to practise as once you have used up your three attempts you must wait 2 years before you can try again.

Revision:

There are several things you can use to help you revise. I have listed below newer editions of the sources that I used:

*   Books:
    *   Teacher's Skills Tests for Dummies UK Edition- Colin Beveridge
    *   Passing the Numeracy Skills Test (Achieving QTS Series) –Mark Patmore
    *   Passing the Literacy Skills Test (Achieving QTS Series)- Jim Johnson
    *   Pass the QTS Numeracy Skills Test with Ease: 2018 – 2020- Vali Nasser
*   Past Papers:
    *   Both online and available to print at http://sta.education. gov.uk. You will need to register to use them.
*   Facebook Groups
    *   Numeracy Ready
    *   Andy GA Palmer
*   Websites
    *   BBC Bitesize

Extra Advice:

*   It is really worth investing time and using resources to prepare for these tests as failing them could cause a two-year delay.

- But don't let it stress you out! My breaking point came after spending eight hours revising for the numeracy test without a break. I had failed my first time and so was very nervous about being locked out. I was actually getting poorer results as the hours went by and I couldn't work out why. Everyone needs a break and some downtime. Schedule a few 1-hour sessions a week but spread them out so you get some time to relax.

- Set up a revision timetable to help you focus on the areas that you struggle with. I would start by taking one of the paper tests and noting down areas I found difficult. I would then mark the paper and write down any areas I thought I needed to revise further. Each week this would be adjusted, and I would add or remove topics as my revision developed. It is important to have clearly defined goals of what you need to achieve in order to make the best use of your time.

Subject Knowledge Enhancement Courses

While not essential for gaining a place on a PGCE course, these extra courses can help you gain academic knowledge of a subject that you have little experience with.

Eligibility:

*   A degree in a topic not related to the course you would like to undertake. For example, you could have a Computing Science degree, but you would like to teach mathematics.
*   Studied a subject for A-Level but not for degree level.
*   Have professional experience but not academic.

Subjects

*   English
*   Mathematics
*   Languages
*   Geography
*   Computing
*   Design and Technology
*   Physics
*   Chemistry
*   Biology

Course Length

There are a few options you can take:

*   Short course- 8 weeks
*   Longer courses- up to 28 weeks

The course can be part-time or full-time, and either online or in person, depending on the institution. You will have to complete an assessment after each unit of study. This could be an essay, example lesson or an exam.

Funding

- The courses are fully funded
- You can get a bursary of £100-£200 for the duration of the course

Apply

- You will need to apply through UCAS once you have been accepted by your provider. It might be worth mentioning your intention to take one of these courses in your personal statement so that the university knows you are looking to improve your skills.

You can find more information about what an SKE course involves through the Get Into Teaching website:

https://getintoteaching.education.gov.uk/
explore-my-options/teacher-training-routes/
subject-knowledge-enhancement-ske-courses/ske-stories

You can also find the providers of these courses on the government website:

https://www.gov.uk/government/publications/
subject-knowledge-enhancement-course-directory

What to Do If You Don't Get Accepted? (Apply 2)

The process is very much like choosing your first three choices, although on this occasion you can only choose one university at a time.

First things first, you need to find vacancies. If you want to check numbers at a specific university, call or email them. They will be busy at this time of year so there may be a small delay. Alternatively, you can search for vacancies on UCAS:

https://www.ucas.com/ucas/teacher-training/
ucas-teacher-training-search-training-programmes

Once you have applied, your new course will show up on Track. As before, the provider has 10 days to get back to you to offer you a place.

Don't worry at this stage: things have a way of working out in the end. Your first three choices were obviously not meant to be.

I would suggest, as you did with your first three choices, that you look carefully at every element of the university, such as transport links and housing, before accepting an offer.

You can keep applying to other universities until one offers you a place.

3
Preparation

*'An investment in knowledge pays
the best interest.'*

Benjamin Franklin

Academic

One thing I can't stress enough is to make sure you have a break. Go on holiday. Lounge around the house. Have a coffee with a few old friends. While on your PGCE, it will become harder (although not impossible) to do these things.

However, I do believe that making a head start will help you in the long run.

Familiarise Yourself with Key Theorists

Every course will have a different approach to teaching, but the fact remains that you will be exposed to a variety of theorists. Researching and making notes about the few theorists and theories I have mentioned below will save you a lot of time later on in the course. Key theories and theorists to research include:

- Constructivism- Piaget
- Social cognition- Vygotsky
- Behaviourism - Skinner
- Learning styles/VARK- Neil Fleming
- Bloom's Taxonomy

You won't be expected to know everything about these theories, but it will be worth becoming familiar with them as they may come up in discussions or essays.

Join Teachers on Social Media

- Facebook has a plethora of teaching pages that you can join
- Twinkle has several pages, ranging from NQT to Supply teaching (and everything in-between)
- Someone normally sets up a PGCE (insert academic year) group which caters to students from various courses
- Fellow students on your course might set up a page for your course so it is worth checking if they have; consider setting up your own if they have not. It is very handy to have one, even if its main use is just to check if lectures are still running.
- TES is another site you should be following to keep up-to-date with current educational news

- Find the teacher union pages: NUT, NASUWT and ATL are the most popular.
- Other sites worth joining include websites where you can buy resources made by teachers

Twitter is also another good place to find advice and resources. I didn't use Twitter myself during my PGCE but other students who did use it found it very helpful. Searching for teachers to follow isn't difficult and there are plenty of articles on the top teachers you should be following. You will also want to follow the union Twitter pages as well for the most up-to-date information.

Teacher blogs are also worth following. TES and Teacher Toolkit were the two I read the most during my PGCE year. Ask your university for recommendations or use a search engine to research the best teaching blogs to follow.

I would also recommend talking to teachers you may know. You could email one of the teachers you had work experience with and ask them for their advice. However, be warned- teachers are busy and so there may be some delay in getting a response.

Read Books and Articles

No doubt your university will have sent you a list of what looks like a hundred books or articles to read. The good news is you don't have to read them all. I chose ten articles and read about broad subjects and made notes on them. SEN, behaviour management, current theories and the latest issues affecting teachers are all good starting points.

Don't waste your money on books- I am speaking from experience!

I love books, and nothing makes me more excited about a course than buying new books. The forums are full of people telling you not to waste money on books and I didn't listen. Needless to say, I believe I spent over £400 over the course of the PGCE.

Were they useful? Some.

Have I kept any of them? Only one.

99% of the books I read made very little impact on me. If you need to get essential books, wait until you start university. But even then, I would hold fire. The library will have a copy of the books on the reading list and you can save a lot of money by photocopying the occasional chapters you need rather than buying the whole book. Most of the 'essential' books I was told to buy were mentioned maybe once in a lecture. I was told to read some books before a lecture which I did. But I became frustrated when the book was not even mentioned, or I could have easily found the same information on the web.

While it is more convenient to have your own copies of books, try the library first if you really must read a certain book. A good proportion of the books I bought were expensive (£15+) and had a shockingly low resale value. So, think carefully before buying books and wasting money.

The only book I did keep and would recommend is called 'Getting the Buggers to Behave' by Sue Cowley. It is a behaviour management book which manages to avoid coming across as too academic. The author is eccentric but also brutally honest. One of the most famous parts of the book is when she eats from a can of dog food (not quite as bad as it seems, but a good trick!) I enjoyed her approaches and ended up using a few of them my class in my second placement.

Files

The PGCE sometimes feels like death by paper. You become terrified of throwing anything away in case you should need it. That's why I suggest setting up files.

You will need the following folders:

- QTS folder:
  This will be something you complete over the year. Each university will have a set way of laying out your folder. I will go into more detail about what to put in the folder in later chapters.
- School Placement One folder:
  Every bit of evidence you collect is eligible for use in your

QTS folder to prove you are on your way to becoming a good teacher.

- Enrichment folder (if your university does it)

Some universities have an enrichment placement in-between placement one and two. You may have to do experience in a sector you are unfamiliar with, such as in a SEN school.

- School Placement Two folder:

Same as for SP1, you will need a second folder to cover your SP2.

- University work folder (with dividers for each class):

This is to keep all lecture notes together. You can use some of your notes in your QTS folder, so it is worth keeping it up to date and neat.

- Miscellaneous folder:

Keep in this folder essays and their subsequent marks, your teacher reference number and any other things that might be useful. For the first part of my course, this miscellaneous folder was a shoe box that contained all the paperwork I didn't want to throw away but didn't know where to put. It took ages to sort out, so I would advise being organised and putting everything in a folder from day one.

Buy a Diary

This is probably one of the most useful things I bought for my PGCE course. Before the course started, I put key dates and birthdays in my diary. The week before each key event, I also put a note to remind me if I needed to buy a present or take something to an event. This was really helpful as sometimes I would be so weighed down with work that I would forget birthdays if I didn't remind myself.

There are diaries to suit all tastes. If you write a lot, I would look at a daily planner, although these can be bigger and heavier than a weekly one. Personally, I prefer a paper diary. I bought a cheap weekly A5 Filofax-style planner from WISH with a pen insert as I am always losing my pens.

Good shops to buy planners from:

- KIKKI-K
- Paper chase
- WHSmith
- Amazon
- eBay
- WISH

You don't have to spend a fortune but try to find a planner that is hardwearing. You might even get a free one when the unions visit your university.

Alternately, you can use an app. Rather than having to carry a planner, the benefit of this is that you can download the app to your phone and it will always be with you. Some good planning apps to try are:

- Trello
- Planner Pro
- The Happiness Planner
- Planner

Unions

It goes without saying, but unions are something you should be a part of while you are a teacher, as well as when you are a student.

The three main unions are: NUS, NASUWT and ATL. Most likely, you will be invited to an event held at the university within a few weeks of starting. As a trainee, you can join as many unions as you like. I'd advise doing this and then, during your training year, decide which suits you best. You will also want to bear in mind which union most of the staff in your NQT school belong to. Should issues arise, you will have more support if you are all part of the same union.

Familiarise Yourself with the Standards

If you haven't heard of the 'standards' yet, don't worry. You will have plenty of time to research them before you start your course.

There are nine standards you need to be familiar with. Each is broken down into smaller sections.

Part One: Teaching

A teacher must:

1. Set high expectations which inspire, motivate and challenge pupils.
2. Promote good progress and outcomes by pupils.
3. Demonstrate good subject and curriculum knowledge.
4. Plan and teach well-structured lessons.
5. Adapt teaching to respond to the strengths and needs of all pupils.
6. Make accurate and productive use of assessment.
7. Manage behaviour effectively to ensure a good and safe learning environment.
8. Fulfil wider professional responsibilities.

Part Two: Personal and Professional Conduct.

*   Teachers should behave in a way that is professional and that maintains high standards for ethics as well as behaviour both in and outside of school.

More details about the standards can be found here: https://www.gov.uk/government/publications/teachers-standards

It is worth researching a few ways you can fulfil each standard before you start university. Most universities require three to five pieces of evidence for each standard. It is important to start working towards the standards as soon as possible. That way you will have more evidence to hand and can cherry pick the best examples that show you are meeting the standards to pass your PGCE.

In later chapters, I will give examples of how to evidence each standard as it is the main method of assessment on the course.

Look for Resources

In the appendix, I include a list of resources I found useful. However, it is always a good idea to have a list of your own preferred resources should you ever be stuck for ideas.

During the period before I started university, I made the following headings in a Word document:

- Resources:
    - Maths
    - English
    - Topic
    - Science
    - PHSE
    - Starters/Plenaries
    - MISC

I made one for both KS1 and KS2 and would drop the name or URLs of any useful resources. You may not know your year group, so it is worth finding resources for a few phases. Facebook and Twitter can be good sources of new ideas.

Home

You've prepared academically, but have you given any thought to how you will cope on the home front? Here are some handy ways to help you prepare.

Get a Calendar

Much like the section about getting a diary, organising your home life is going to make things 100% easier. Include things like dentist, doctor and optician appointments, as well as key dates for insurance. Also, schedule time for birthdays (include reminders for presents) and other special events. You need time away from teaching; make sure you have fun things to do with family and friends written down, so you remember to do them!

Get Essential Appointments Booked

When you get into the swing of things, you will resent spending a Saturday morning in a waiting room. The appointments you'll want to book are:

- Optician
- Check up with the dentist. Also, if you need any work done on your teeth, consider doing it before the course begins.
- A doctor's appointment to make sure you have the relevant prescriptions you need. It will be very difficult (unless an emergency) to schedule appointments during school hours.

Sort Routines

- How long will it take you to get to university each morning? What bus/train will you need to catch? When will you cook/ clean/do the washing? Try and work out a rough routine of what you need to do and when you can fit it in. I didn't want to spend 3 hours doing washing at the weekend, so I would do it on a Thursday evening while I got on with work or did my food shopping.
- Try to find ways of fitting jobs into the small gaps of time you have so you aren't wasting huge chunks of your day on tasks. Cooking double portions to save yourself cooking every day is

just one example. Cooking two meals takes no more time than cooking one.

- Tip: planning meals will not only save you time, but also money. I have included some quick meals in the appendix to help you on those days when you really can't be bothered to cook.

Social Media

- Locking down your social media is an absolute essential! Whether it's Twitter, Facebook, Tumblr or Instagram, if it displays your real name or anything that could identify you, change your name or the settings. The last thing you will want is to have parents or students seeing what you got up to at the weekend.

- A common way to deal with names on a site like Facebook is to remove a surname or change the spelling. For example:

  o Full name: Louise Jane Smith

     You could use:

     Louise Jane

     Louise Jones (if a common name, even better)

     Jane Louise

     Lou Jane

- Make sure only people on your friends list can see what you post. You can also change your settings to make it difficult for companies like Google to put you in their search results.

Clothing

Unless you love spending hours at the weekend washing and ironing, these will become jobs you just don't have time for (unless you have a very sympathetic family!) My solution is to simplify your wardrobe- the less decorative the better.

I lived away from home for my PGCE and resented washing as I had to go to a laundrette. At first, I would spend ages in the morning trying to choose an outfit; I knew I needed to make my life as easy as possible in this department so I started to limit my outfit choices. I stocked up on items from Matalan, Peacocks and Primark as I didn't want to spend a lot on clothes that could be ruined by sticky hands. An example of a capsule wardrobe for both men and women that would require washing only once every two weeks would be:

Women

- 1 black cardigan/ 1 coloured cardigan
- 10 t-shirts (plain colours work best)
- 3 bottoms (trousers, skirts or long shorts- air between uses)
- 2 pairs of smart shoes
- A few pairs of tights or leggings
- A smart coat
- A strong, durable business bag and canvas/plastic bags to carry books
- A P.E. kit (T-shirt, trousers, jumper and shoes)

Men

- 10 shirts
- 3 ties to go with the shirts
- 3 trouser suits
- 2 pairs of smart shoes
- A smart coat
- A strong, durable bag and canvas/plastic bags to carry books
- A P.E. kit (T-shirt, trousers, jumper and shoes)

Obviously, you need to get what works for you, but I'd advise against wearing your best clothes to work as they will get dirty or ruined. A lovely Year One child once asked why I had 'poo' on my back; it turned out that I had sat in brown paint due to someone leaving their work to dry on a chair (this thankfully came out in the wash).

Other Key Items to Have

- Printer
  - o There is no denying it, you will be printing a lot of paperwork and resources. Now, you can do all of this at school or university. It is do-able. However, I am sure you'll find it much easier to have your own printing device.

- o   Before buying a printer, have a look at the reviews online. The last thing you are going to want is an unreliable printer- you'll meet plenty of those at school.
- o   Look at how much ink will cost you as some cheap printers demand very expensive ink. I enrolled with HP Instant Ink while in university as it only cost £7.99 a month and I could have up to 300 pages of colour or black and white printing. The printer even ordered the ink for me when I was running low, so I didn't have to make a mad dash to a shop to buy ink.
- o   If you are going to spend the money on a new printer, I would also look for one that has a scanning function. I found this very helpful when adding information to my QTS file.
- • USB stick/ Hard drive/ back up system
  - o   For day to day use, I recommend buying a small USB stick to carry around with you. I bought one with a fairly large capacity of 64GB as I had a lot of files on my device.
  - o   I had bought a hard drive before university to store home movies and important documents, but this was also very helpful for backing up school work. I would use my PPA on a Friday to make sure all my work was backed up before I left.
  - o   As an extra precaution, make sure you back up your work somewhere else, such as on the Cloud. Dropbox or OneDrive worked very well for me and allowed me to access my files from anywhere. Alternatively, if it was a very important file, I would email it to myself to make sure I always had a copy to hand.
- • Laptop
  - o   Now this will be a personal choice. You will have access to computers at school and university. My first placement didn't even have a PPA room, so I was forced to bring my own laptop to school, transfer files to my USB stick, and then print them at the end of the day. It wasn't ideal, but I was glad I had my own laptop.
  - o   I bought a small HP Stream laptop (a bit like a Chrome Book). It only had 32GB of storage, but as I stored everything externally, it did not matter. I was even able

to load Microsoft Office onto it (although you can use a version online if you have a Hotmail email account). I couldn't load any intensive software such as iTunes so, for this reason, I would not have used it as my only laptop. However, as it was cheap, I had the reassurance of knowing that if a child did break it, I hadn't lost hundreds of pounds.

o   Several people on my course had Macs and they coped well. As you can use Microsoft Office packages, they were easily able to switch between software. One thing to bear in mind is that you may not be able to get some school software on your Mac.

• Guillotine/laminator

o   If you are in the lower key stages of a primary school, you will be cutting and laminating most of your resources. You can get a guillotine and a laminator for around £20 in shops like The Range or WHSmith. If you know you are going to be doing a lot at home, invest in a more expensive item as most of the more expensive products allow you to cut/laminate more pages at a time than the cheaper ones.

Items to Take If You Are Moving Away from Home:

I decided to move away to study and I am sad to say I made many of the packing pitfalls you are advised against. Five different pans, four sets of plates, and boxes of cleaning products were not really needed and just took up valuable space in my small room. In hindsight, I should have just taken the bare minimum of stuff and then bought the rest when I got to my room. Here is a list of things I actually used:

• Kitchen

o   Saucepan

o   Frying pan

o   Small set of cutlery

o   2 plates and bowls

o   2 Glass or plastic cups

o   2 mugs

o   Chopping board

- o   Knives
- o   Spatula
- o   Scissors
- o   Kettle/toaster (if allowed/not supplied)
- o   Cleaning supplies (dish soap, sponges, cleaning products)
- Bathroom
  - o   Loo roll
  - o   Shampoo/conditioner
  - o   Razors/shaving foam
  - o   Shower gel
  - o   Small boxes to store make-up/toiletries
  - o   Medical kit
- Bedroom
  - o   Lamp
  - o   Bedding
  - o   Duvet/pillows
  - o   Personal items (pictures, fairy lights etc.)
  - o   Clothes (see previous list)
- Office
  - o   Paper
  - o   Printer
  - o   Laptop
  - o   Chargers
  - o   USB/ Hard drive
  - o   Small pencil case
  - o   Pens
  - o   Work bag
  - o   PGCE files
  - o   Expandable wallet (to store lesson plans in)
  - o   Heavy duty bag for books
- Paperwork
  - o   ID- birth certificate, driving license or passport
  - o   Course details

o   Important addresses

o   Calendar/ diary

This is by no means a comprehensive list. However, if I had just stuck to this basic list, I wouldn't have ended up taking two car loads worth of stuff with me.

Advice If You Are Moving from Home

•   Take photos when you move in; many students have been stung by charges for damage caused by previous tenants before they moved in.

•   Give everything a deep clean. I spent an hour deep cleaning things when I moved in as it made it feel more like my place.

•   Don't forget to change your address. You may need proof you live at your new address in situations such as taking out a new phone contract or registering with a local doctor.

Student Money

Student Finance

In the previous chapter, I gave a rough idea of what you can expect to receive financially during your course. The final deadline to apply for Student Finance is fairly generous but the sooner you do it, the better. Rushing around to find more information to send to them just before the deadline is going to stress you out. Applications tend to open around February/March, but it is best to check on the Student Finance page website for the exact opening and closing dates for your location.

You will want to set aside an hour to fill in the form as you do not want to have it sent back to you due to an error. Depending on your age, you'll need your parents' or partner's income information as this will help Student Finance to assess your entitlement. Your income assessment will be based on your income during the previous tax year.

The form can be completed online or on paper. I have always found the paper options take longer to be processed, but it's up to you to choose the method you are most comfortable with. Evidence may need to be sent to corroborate the information entered on the form. If you have to send originals, make sure you take photocopies in case they get lost.

Student Banking

Something that I highly recommend is a student bank account. You will usually be offered a free overdraft which means you will not pay fees should you go overdrawn. You may also be offered a credit card with a small limit. Only accept the credit card if you know you are good with money; do not use it to cover bills etc. as you will be charged high fees. One advantage of having a credit card is the protection it offers. The Consumer Credit Act (1974) Section 75, protects you for any purchase from £100 to £30,000 bought using your credit card. You also don't have to pay for the whole thing on your credit card. This means if you buy a £900 laptop and put £100 of the cost on a credit card, you are protected for the whole £900. This is good for things like holidays or if an item breaks and a retailer will not fix it.

Check if your current bank offers a student account but be prepared to switch if not. Some banks will also offer you good incentives, such as free travel cards. Obviously, you shouldn't pick an account based on this alone, but it is nice to have these things for free if you will use them or were going to buy them anyway.

Budgeting

The best way to save money is to budget. You need to set aside an amount for anything you buy/use each month and stick to it.

An example budget for a student living in a London house share might look like this:

Total income:
Student Finance: £12,000
Savings from work: £1000
Birthday/Christmas money: £250

So, your total income over the year will be £13,250. This works out at £1,204.54 per month for eleven months.

Monthly outgoings:
Rent: £400
Utilities: £25
Internet: £11.50
Mobile: £30
Food: £200
Entertainment/presents: £75
Insurance: £10
Laundry: £14
Toiletries: £15
Clothes: £20
University books: £5
Ink/paper: £7.99
Printing at university: £2.00

The monthly outgoings amount to £815.49.

£1,204.54- £815.49= £389.05

£389.05 is your surplus each month. You can use this as savings or to pay for anything not listed in your budget. There may also be a delay in you getting a job once you leave so it is always helpful to have some money spare. Do bear in mind that payments from Student Finance can arrive late or halfway through a month. When you get your statement from Student Finance, it will outline when you will be paid; this should help you budget for the coming months.

Monthly costs will vary depending on where you live in the country and whether you house share or live in halls. Some costs might not be needed every month, like clothes or books. In these cases, it is best to work out the total cost per year and then divide it by the months you are in university. For example:

Books: £200
Months in university :11
200/11=£18.11 per month.

It will be hard to stick to a budget if it is not realistic. To make sure it is still working for you, it is wise to regularly check the amounts in your budget should you need to lower or increase them.

Jobs

Several people on my PGCE course boosted their income with part-time jobs. The decision to work alongside studying will most likely be determined by your financial situation. It is not impossible to work, but you will need to be highly organised. If you feel money may be very tight during your PGCE, it might be worth considering taking a gap year and working to save money. I worked for an agency as a teaching assistant in my gap year to gain extra experience.

If you would like a job that can work around your studies, then tutoring could be the answer. You can choose the hours you are available and reduce them if you are finding time harder to juggle. Depending on your area, you could earn between £10-£30 an hour.

Money Saving Tips:

- Join MoneySavingExpert.com. The guy who set up the site, Martin Lewis, appears regularly on TV offering tips to save money. The forum has a dedicated student money saving page which I found invaluable. You can also subscribe to weekly emails which tell you about upcoming deals.

- Get a NUS card. From 30% off at Zizzi to 10% at Warehouse, you can save so much with it. Lots of stores will also accept your regular student ID. You can also sign up to Myunidays. com where they will register you and give you discount codes to use online or in store. I used this app when buying my computer and saved around 10%.

- Check if you are eligible for extra funding. If you are on a low income, some universities have discretionary funds to help you. Student Finance also has extra money available for those who have children or who are disabled.

- Reduce costs. Go through your bank account and see if you can cancel memberships you do not use.

- Buy books from eBay or Amazon. Don't buy books unless essential; go to the library instead. Bookbutler.com can help you search for the cheapest books.

- Full-time students do not have to pay council tax. If you are living at home with other people who are not students, the council tax will be reduced to account for the fact you are not eligible.

- Shop at budget stores like ALDI or LIDL. They have smaller ranges, but they tend to be cheaper.

- Use comparison sites to check bills. Sites like USWITCH can help you drastically reduce your bills. Comparethemarket offers the extra incentive of 2for1 cinema tickets if you take out certain polices.

- If you know you will have money spare at the end of the month, set up a direct debit to transfer this to a savings account so you don't spend it.

- If you have to call a premium number, such as an 0870 number, use the website/app Saynoto08700 to make the call cheaper.

- Get a student rail/bus/oyster card.

- Pay for your TV license monthly. Alternatively, if you pay annually, you can get some money back when you leave.

- Check if you are owed tax from jobs you did before university.

- Need household items? Try local Facebook groups or your local Freecycle.
- Discount coffee? Some cafes will give you a small discount if you bring your own mug.
- Hair and beauty treatments can be obtained cheaply if you go to local colleges. I had a decent hair cut at a local college salon for £5. It did take longer, but there was a tutor around to help with any issues.

4
University

'Education is not preparation for life; education is life itself.'

John Dewy

Why Do I Need to Go to University?

At the start of your course, you're probably going to be feeling nervous. While you will spend longer on your teaching placements than at university, the time you do spend at university is key to helping you develop your knowledge. Here, you will have the opportunity to learn and trial teaching theories in a safe and constructive way. However, you will be expected to do a fair amount of work outside of university hours to reap the most benefits.

Initially, I found the university section of the course tedious. The lectures seemed to drag, and I really didn't see how drawing pictures in chalk in a carpark had anything to do with teaching English well. But that is the point of university: to try new things. Trust me, it is much better to try something a little 'way out' at university and have it go horribly wrong there than have it go horribly wrong in front of 30 unrelenting children. At university, you'll have the chance to ask lecturers (who have taught for years) their advice on how to improve. I didn't really appreciate university until after my first placement. Only then did the theories and methods we had been taught start to make sense.

The best way to handle university is to treat it like a job. You have set hours, usually between 9am and 5pm, although you may have to come in earlier/stay later on occasions. Don't be tempted to skip classes as your attendance is monitored and used to inform your reference.

You will have a mixture of subject-based lessons, such as mathematics, and theory-based lessons focusing on professional studies. Your main assignments will most likely be around these topics, so take detailed notes and try not to miss classes.

My main piece of advice to you is to enjoy your time at university. Enjoy getting up 'late' or being able to pop to the coffee shop between lectures. You will enjoy having no marking to take home, I promise you that! Before you know it, it will be over and you'll be back in a school. So, enjoy being a student and try to digest as much as possible. It will help you enormously in placements.

QTS and the PGCE

Did you know that there are two PGCEs? The Post Graduate Certificate of Education and the Professional Graduate Certificate in Education.

Does the route you take to train to become a teacher have any impact on employability? The simple answer is no.

Most universities will offer the postgraduate option as default. This means that you will earn some Master's credits should you ever want to complete a postgraduate course. It also means that your essays will be graded at postgraduate level, as opposed to undergraduate. When I was at university and submitted assignments, you would initially be graded at Master's level. If you didn't quite pass the first time, you had the chance to resubmit at Master's level again. If you still didn't quite make it, you were graded at an undergraduate level instead. If both assignments passed at postgraduate level, you would be awarded Master's credits (usually 60) and the Postgraduate Certificate. If one or both essays didn't pass, then you would not get the Master's credits and would be awarded the Professional Graduate Certificate.

QTS, or Qualified Teacher Status, is something you will most likely hear on a daily basis. It is the award you need to be able to teach in maintained state schools or non-maintained specialist schools in England and Wales. Maintained schools are schools funded by the local authority. If you trained outside of England and Wales, you can easily apply for QTS to be able to teach in these areas. It normally takes around a month for your application to be processed. More information can be found here:

https://www.gov.uk/guidance/
qualified-teacher-status-qts#teachers-who-trained-in-england

There are many routes to gaining QTS and you do not need to have a PGCE to teach. Once you finish your PGCE, your training provider will recommend you for QTS. If you have done well, you will be granted QTS. You then need to complete three terms as an NQT (Newly Qualified Teacher) which is a sort of probationary period of teaching. If you do not complete your NQT successfully, you cannot teach in maintained schools. You can, however, teach in privately-run schools as they do not require you to have QTS. You will have to prove you meet the teaching standards as you do for the PGCE, but how you do this will vary depending on your local authority.

First Days

Whenever you start something new, it's normal to feel trepidation. The PGCE requires a lot of information to be absorbed and can be daunting at first. If you are organised, you might have a list of questions you would like answered, or even a list of things to do in the first few days.

You will not know everything immediately- you have to understand that. Reassuringly, every other student will be in the same situation. The best way to deal with the PGCE is to just let things roll over you. I made the mistake of trying to rush to get to know things and it just became frustrating; lecturers, schools and admin staff will do things in their own time. You are not, and will not be, the first student they have had. It took me a few months but I learned eventually to just let things roll. You'll stress out too much if you don't which isn't healthy.

Below is a list of things to try and sort out in the first week to make things run smoothly.

- Introduction lectures
  - o Close to your starting date, you should receive an email with a timetable of what needs to be done and when in the first week. You might have scheduled talks on:
    - Meeting the lecturers
    - Well-being
    - What to expect
    - Essays
    - What lectures you will have
    - Course structure
    - What to do if something goes wrong
  - o You may also get a course handbook. It is worth bringing a notebook and pen to help you remember everything- there will be a lot of information!
- Council tax exemption and voting.
  - o If you are eligible, you can get a reduction in council tax. The local council will inform you about what you need to do to prove this. The sooner you do this, the faster you will save money. If there is an election scheduled for when

you are in university, make sure you are on the electoral roll as you will not be eligible to vote otherwise.

- Student Finance registration
  - o Some universities will schedule this in and combine it with getting your student ID. It can take some time to receive your first Student Finance payment as the university needs to prove you are actually attending. This is something you will want to sort out as soon as you can.

- Admin
  - o Your university might schedule a library tour, as well as a tour of the computer facilities. If offered, do attend as you'll appreciate knowing the systems and where things are come essay submission time.

  - o You'll want to set up your university email quickly as this is how the university will contact you. You might be able to keep the email address a few months after you leave university, but it is always a good idea to have a professional separate email address as well. Sexibabbi200 is just not going to send the right message to potential employers.

  - o Email accounts are also a good way of backing up information. I used to send important essays or pieces of work to myself via email. It was also good for storing useful ideas or pictures.

- Paperwork
  - o Even before you start the PGCE, you will have a ton of paperwork. Not all of it is immediately useful. Get into the habit of sorting your work as soon as you get home. As mentioned in the previous chapter, you should have five folders already set up: QTS, SE1+Enrichment, SE2, University Work and MISC.

  - o Start filing as soon as you can. Everything you file can be used in your QTS folder. You should be familiar with the standards now, so when filing, put a small note in the top corner of which standards it could be used for. I did this throughout my time at university and it only took me two hours to sort my file at the end of the course.

  - o Don't put anything in your QTS file. You don't need to yet. But labelling will save you so much time at the end when you are teaching an 80% timetable.

Lessons

- Subject Knowledge
  - One of the biggest misconceptions about the lectures you will attend on school topics is that they are designed to teach you about the topic. The truth is they aren't. Not good at maths? Your lecturer is not going to be giving you lessons on understanding algebra. They will, however, teach you how to deliver it. That's not to say your tutors won't help if you are struggling, but it is expected that you learn outside of the classroom. The good news is anything you produce (notes, workings out etc.) that show you are trying to improve your skills can be put in your QTS folder for standard three. In some lectures, you may expect you to complete directed activities, such as summarising a theory or designing a lesson plan. I will go into more detail later about the types of directed activities you can expect.
  - You will most likely have weekly lectures for core subjects such as mathematics, English and science. Other subjects, such as PE, history or art, might just be focused on once per block of university time.
  - Lectures can be a mixed bag. I've had really interesting lectures. For example, in history, we once had to go and find out about the area around the university by asking local people. However, I've also been to lectures where I have had to sit and listen to a lecturer drone on endlessly, with the occasional group work task thrown in to keep it interesting. It does make you appreciate how your students must feel. The engaging lessons also give you plenty of ideas to try when you have your own class.
  - You will learn about the key theories of each subject, as well as ways in which to deliver it. You might be expected to attend a lecture given by a guest speaker or present ideas of your own to your class. For mathematics, my class once had to design a mini-lesson for a group of six children which would be repeated four times. I couldn't understand at the time how this was relevant. After all, how much could I teach in ten minutes? But we were encouraged to reflect after every group which gave us

time to see what worked and what didn't. It also taught us how much you can actually teach someone in ten minutes if you choose to focus carefully on one objective.

- Specialism Subjects (Curriculum Studies)

  o Depending on your university, you might be offered a choice specialisms. My options were Modern Languages, Children's Literature, Early Years Education or Mathematics Action Research. Being an English graduate, I desperately wanted to study the literature module but, unfortunately, I was allocated Modern Languages. Initially, I was disappointed. I was the only person in the class who did not know a foreign language (pre-GCSE French will only get you so far) and I felt very isolated.

    However, I ended up actually enjoying it. I had been meaning to learn French for a while and this gave me a good excuse. Every night I would practise my French on the Duolingo app and research the words I was unsure about. The lecturer of this class was really supportive and encouraging; when you start teaching, you'll come to see how much of a difference this can make to students' engagement in a class. The lecturer had learnt several languages which meant she could understand the frustration of someone learning a new language. Being able to put yourself in your student's shoes will help you understand how best to help them. This is one of the softer skills I learnt from this tutor, but a very valuable one.

    As part of a directed activity, I had to teach a 20-minute French lesson. If you had told me a year before that I would be teaching French to six-year-olds, I would have laughed. I even did fairly well on my assignment and still continue with my French lessons today.

    What I am trying to say, in a rather long-winded way, is keep an open mind. What at first seems bad can actually turn out rather well. You might even find a new passion.

    As part of my course, I had to complete an assignment on my specialism. Not all courses will expect this and may instead require you to do an assignment on another area. If you do get the option, it is worth undertaking an assignment in a specialist subject. Not only are you unlikely to have the chance again to spend time researching an area you are interested in, but it may also help you should you want to become Head of a department later on in your career, or even complete a Master's degree. Tasks you might be asked to do could include teaching a small class, interviewing a Head of Department, planning a starter for a class, or completing a research assignment.

- SPIRE:
  o SPIRE (Studies in Professional Issues and Research in Education) may be called something different on your course but the general topic remains the same. The role of SPIRE is to bridge the relationship between theories that affect education and the practical side of teaching.

  o There are several things that can affect a student's outcome in school. These include:
    - SEN
    - Gender
    - Race and ethnicity
    - EAL
    - Refuge/migrant status.

  o These are, of course, very broad headings. Children may even fall into more than one category. Being aware of issues that can hinder children in their education will enable you to try and accommodate them and help them to progress.

  o One example that made me really focus on what I was delivering in class was when the discussion of refugees. Subjects in the curriculum may make the child become upset. Teaching a book about WWII and the bombing of London could trigger a distressing memory if the child has been in a country where this has happened. These children may also be unable to speak much English and so could struggle to articulate problems. As a teacher, you need to be aware of these sorts of issues and how to deal with them.

o   To cement our knowledge of this subject, a 4000-5000-word assignment was set. You had to choose a child who you identified as fitting into one of the categories listed above and conduct a child study on them. After conducting research into our chosen topic area, we then were required to critically evaluate the evidence based on the behaviours the child exhibited. While you can't do this for every child in your class, keeping up-to-date on research and how to implement it in your classroom is an essential skill.

- Professional Studies:

o   Much like SPIRE, PS covers topics that are not curriculum based. The aim of Professional Studies is to equip you with the professional knowledge and understanding you will need to become a reflective practitioner.

o   You will mostly be focusing on issues that will affect you as a professional, such as:

- E-Safety
- Prevent
- Behaviour Management
- Safeguarding
- Assessment
- Data

o   You might also look at learning theories and other more theoretical ideas. One of the most interesting parts of my university experience was having guest lectures come in to discuss these topics. Having the opportunity to ask questions and meet people who had already experienced these issues and could offer advice was invaluable.

o   It is important to attend these sessions. Information gets updated all the time and it is only by attending these sessions that you can gain the most up-to-date information in regard to policies.

Coursework

- Assignments
  - Some courses will require you to complete several small essays of around 1000-1500 words. Other courses may require you to complete two larger assessments. If your course offers Master's credits, you will need to submit 10,000 words in total; how this is divided up is decided by the university.
  - For my course, I had to complete two 5000-word essays. I won't go into too much detail about how to write these essays as they will vary from course to course. There are also some amazing books available to buy (or loan) which detail how to write outstanding essays.
  - The first essay was a child study. I had to choose a subject from my SPIRE lessons and conduct both a literature review and a case study on a child (completed mostly via observation and discussions with the child, parent or teacher). The aim was to teach us how to look out for issues that might affect a student's learning and learn how a teacher can adapt their teaching to help. While I can't write 5000 words on every child, the process of observing and researching is a skill I used later on in my teaching career whenever a child wasn't making the expected rate of progress.
  - The second essay was based on my chosen specialist subject (MFL). I had to conduct a literature review on an element of teaching MFL to primary school children. I also had to teach a small MFL lesson based on the evidence of the literature review.
  - Both essays were based on topics covered in lectures, so I had a good starting point.
  - 5000 words sounds very scary when you are first told about it but breaking the topic down into smaller, easier parts will help. You should be given an assessment grid in order to see how you can achieve your desired target grade.
  - Once you have decided on a title, you should start scheduling research periods into your week. The library

is an obvious place to start and most libraries allow you to order books online and collect later which will help to save time. Articles are also a good source of information so keep safe any you are given during lectures.

o   After you have found all your sources, you will need to sort them. I found choosing two books or articles per scheduled session and then writing notes on them more achievable than making notes on a huge pile of different texts. Make sure you write down the name of the book and all the reference information you will need. If I only needed a short part of the book, I would photocopy the front cover and the pages I needed so I could easily carry it around and make notes when I had a spare few minutes. You can always look up information online (or use Amazon's 'look inside' feature which is helpful for publishing details).

o   When you have all your notes, you can start making an essay plan. I always found writing a rough estimate of how much to include in each section helped me to keep on track.

o   If you are not good at referencing, there are good sites to help you with this. One website I used a lot during my PGCE was Neil's Toolbox. You just drop in the information you need, and it will create a reference for you.

o   Make sure you leave yourself time to edit and submit your work. Don't assume everything will go to schedule. If you get sick, you could lose a week. Always start early and build in extra time; it is better to be ahead than behind.

•   APs

o   As with many things in this chapter, the way in which students are assessed is decided by each individual university. One type of assessment is an AP (Assessment Phase) document. It is a document that lists each of the teaching standards and numbers 1 (outstanding evidence of the standard) to 4 (failing to meet the standard). It is a self-appraisal document that students fill in as well as their tutors. This gives a student and their mentor an idea of how they are progressing and what they need to do to improve further. You may not always agree with your mentors and they may not agree with you. I highly recommend taking the time before your tutor meetings to write notes, so you can direct the tutor to why you feel you are at that particular grade point.

o   Don't worry if you have a low score initially; it gives you areas in which to improve and show progress. You can also use observations to help you fill out the document. The emphasis is on you being able to prove you have hit that target. No one will have a problem with you rating yourself as outstanding in your first term, as long as you have strong evidence to support your claim. You complete the AP form just before the end of every assessment phase, so around three times over the course of the year.

- Pen Portraits

o   Much like an AP, a pen portrait is designed to show your progress at a given time and will be completed just before you go to SE2.

o   It is a self-appraisal form and is designed to help you see what you have achieved and what you have left to accomplish to pass the course.

o   Sections you may have to fill in are:

  - Current level of achievement

  - Experience prior to starting the PGCE

  - What you did in SE1

  - What you did in Enrichment

  - First assignment grades

  - Self-assessment of confidence in teaching certain subjects

  - Priority targets for SE2

o   While these forms can seem to take forever, they do have their uses, such as helping you to fill in your induction profile. Personally, I also found it beneficial to be able to write down all I had achieved and see that I didn't have much further to go. This is especially helpful when you've had a bad day.

- Reflective Diary
  - o   Not all universities will ask you to complete a reflective diary but even if they don't, it might be worth setting up your own.
  - o   The diary requires you to choose targets at the beginning of the week and write notes on how you are working towards them. At the end of the week, you review your progress and have your mentor write their own comments on your development.
  - o   Anything you write can be used as evidence in your folder. Sometimes, it will all seem a little pointless and like you are wasting time, but by taking the time to write notes about your progress you are able to reflect on your learning. Abstract concepts will become relevant and you will notice this in your lessons. Being able to see how far you've come will also give you something to be proud of.
- Directed Tasks
  - o   In order to help you prove you are completing the standards, you may be required to complete 'directed tasks' for coursework. These tasks will be related to the standards and are meant to give you some extra evidence to use in your folder.
  - o   On my course, I had to complete three sets of directed tasks: one for SE1, one for Enrichment and one for SE2. The tasks set for SE1 and SE2 were similar, and in some cases identical. You might be asked to write notes on the school's behaviour policy and how you might implement it in class. Alternatively, you could be asked to show how you have adapted your lessons for SEN children in your class.
  - o   Try to complete these tasks early on when you have little planning to complete. I left the tasks until quite late in my first placement and ended up working most weekends. In my second placement, I had completed most of the tasks within the first month. I was much more relaxed as a result.

- Directed Time
    - When you are an NQT, you will be given an 80% timetable, compared to a 90% timetable as a fully qualified teacher. 10% of this extra time will be used to complete your QTS folder in the form of courses, filing paperwork or observations. The other 10% will be your PPA time. Try not to use your extra QTS folder time to plan lessons as you will not have this time once you are fully qualified.
    - Obviously, while at university, you won't be planning like you will be while at school. Nonetheless, you will be given time off in the week to complete extra work. It is a good opportunity to learn to learn to manage your time. Some weeks you may only get one session off, others you may get two. It depends on your schedule.
    - Use this time effectively. Plan what you need to do for each session and aim to only plan what you can realistically complete. This means breaking down tasks into smaller chunks. I found writing my intentions at the beginning of the week made completing all my tasks so much easier as I knew exactly what I needed to do. It's a great feeling to know you are ahead and it gives you a buffer should you need to take time off for whatever reason. Being organised is key here.
- Notes on Directed Time
    - While at university, you will be given directed time off. This is usually two sessions a week, much like you will have on placements as an NQT. It is to give you time to complete work for university, not an excuse for a lie-in every week. Depending on how you work best, you can work at home or at university. Don't be tempted to waste the time as you will regret it later on. That being said, sometimes we all need a break. There were a few occasions after I had worked all weekend when I would take the directed time off to do something non-university related, such as go to the cinema or catch up on a TV series. Being overstressed will not help you, nor will it make your work better. Treat university like a job where you have set hours to work or, if that doesn't work, at

least set a weekly limit for yourself. At the beginning, I regularly pushed myself to do 70 hours of work a week which wasn't sustainable and nearly made me leave the course. Too much pressure is not good for you.

o   One way I kept track of all the work I had to do was to make a tracker on Excel. At the beginning of the course, I inputted every deadline I needed to meet. Every month I would then write down what I had to complete that month in order to meet the deadline by breaking the work down into small chunks. If it was an assignment, I might even start six weeks ahead to make sure I had plenty of time. You will need to be organised for this system to work and also be realistic. If Christmas is coming up, don't try and schedule the same amount of work that you would for a normal month- it just won't happen.

o   I have included an example of the tracker in the appendix to help you get started.

5
Placements

'It is the mark of an educated mind to be able to entertain a thought without accepting it.'

Aristotle

Your Placement

Depending on how your course is run, you may find out about your placement within a few weeks of starting. All students are incredibly anxious to know their school so they can find out a little about it. However, even if you know the name of the school, you might struggle to find out what it's like. Once you come to your second placement, it should be easier as you will have other students to ask.

Don't be afraid to request a particular age range or type of school. If done early enough (before the course starts), it shouldn't be a problem. You can also approach a school and arrange it yourself.

To help you prepare for your school, you will need to do the following:

- Get details from the university:
  - You will need the address, phone number and email of the person to contact at the school (this will normally be your mentor). Call fairly promptly after receiving the details to introduce yourself. Your university may also ask you to send a letter to the school to let them know a little bit about yourself. If you feel nervous, write down what you would like to know, such as:
    - Dress code
    - School start and end time
    - Parking
    - If you should you bring anything with you (paperwork etc.)
    - Your class and a little about them. For example, SEN students, behaviour issues, or any other known issues you need to be aware of.
  - Make sure you save this person's contact details as they will be your first point of call.
  - The university may also let you know who your tutor will be.

- Research:
  - o Once you have the name of the school, it is worth doing some research.
    - ▪ OFSTED:

      If you go to the OFSTED website you can find out the rating of the school. This also shows where schools can make improvements, so you can get a good idea of what the school might be focusing on when you are there.

    - ▪ School website:

      Next, you will want to look at the school website. What is the school's ethos? Do they list what the children are currently studying? Do they run any after-school activities you'd like to help with? You might also be able to see the faces of some staff members which can make meeting them less daunting.

    - ▪ General search:

      Type the school into Google and see what comes up. Has the school appeared in the local paper? Is there a Netmum's group? Are they planning on extending the school? All these things may seem trivial, but they give you a sense of where the school has come from and where they want to end up.

Your First Days

Your first few days are going to be scary. If you have done your research, it should be a little less daunting.

- What to Wear:
  - o Until you know the dress code, play it safe: black skirt/ trousers with either a shirt or simple t-shirt for women, and a suit for men. You can always become less formal but it's best to make a good first impression.
  - o Some schools have looser dress codes and allow options such as jeans and leggings. I would recommend dressing formally for the first week and observe what the other staff are wearing. Then, the following week, make the change to less formal.
- Go to the Staff Room:
  - o At break, go to the staff room! On your first day, try taking some sweets or a tub of biscuits as these are always appreciated and can get a conversation started- even if it is only a debate about the best dunking biscuit!
  - o You may not always have time, but try to go a few times a week, even just to grab a cup of tea and have a quick chat about the weather. Staff in the school will be invaluable to you as they have years of advice. As long as you don't catch someone in a rush, most staff are happy to offer advice when they can.
- Get to Know Your Teacher/Tutor/Staff
  - o Try to make an effort to learn names. If the school website has pictures of staff members, try practising at home. People are far more likely to warm to you if you make the effort to learn their name.
  - o Your tutor should visit you within a few weeks of starting at the school. Find out the best way to contact them as some tutors may prefer texting over an email. Once you have started, there is no harm is emailing your tutor to ask when your first meeting will be and to say you've settled in.
  - o You will be spending most of the time with your class teacher so try to get along with him/her even if you don't see eye to eye. Ask about their experience or if they have a specialism. You should also try to be helpful. You will

soon realise as a teacher that you appreciate someone who just gets on with it. Offer to photocopy or do playground duty occasionally as the little things help and mean the teacher is more likely to want to help you back.

- Mentor Meeting

  o Within the first week, try to arrange to meet your mentor. If they are a busy person, this might be early in the morning or late at night. Try to be flexible as schools are very busy places and trying to fit in a meeting might take some time.

  o If you have any forms, try to have them ready to go to reduce wasted time. It will also be beneficial to have some goals to work towards that you can discuss.

- Get to Know Your Class

  o Probably the scariest thing will be meeting your class. Thirty staring eyes watching you suspiciously was how I felt. Here are some tips to help you settle in:

    ▪ Greet the children each morning. Ask what they did at the weekend or that evening. Try to keep a note of what each child said. The first few days of my placement were lonely as none of the children really answered anything more than 'it was okay.' Eventually, after around a week, they started to open up. Even on a full timetable, I made sure I did this each morning as I found the children liked it and it built up a bond. If you are on duty, you can also have these chats to find out what they like. Finding out what they are interested in can help you to plan really engaging lessons based on their interests.

    ▪ When talking to a child, bend down to their level. Children won't feel as intimidated and I found the children were more engaged.

    ▪ Try a fact game. This is where you throw a ball and you have to introduce yourself by name and give a fact about yourself if you catch it. The children like to hear about you and also like to share information about themselves.

    ▪ Don't sit and watch, join in. As you will soon be teaching these children, they need to see you as a teacher, not an observer. Help them with their work and move around as this will give you an insight into the children's levels which will help with planning.

How to Join In

There are several ways to contribute to school life:

- Run a Club:
  - o One of the easiest ways to join in is to offer to run a club either at lunch or after school. You can offer to help with an existing club or set up your own. You can use this for your standards (3,4,8 and part 2) and it will help you to get to know your pupils. Some example clubs you could offer are: craft, reading, sport, chess, film, sewing, games or drawing.
- Sports/Event Days:
  - o If you are available, attend events or offer to help out. Helping to run a book fair or collect money for the Christmas fair is always appreciated and helpful. Again, it can also be used for part 2 of the standards.
- Meetings
  - o Attend all meetings if you can. You are, while at school, a member of staff and should act like one. Meetings do tend to drag on so be prepared. I always took some work to do while I was waiting for people to arrive. Join in during discussions and group work even if you are unsure. Don't be afraid to ask questions if you don't understand a technical term.

Tutor and Mentor Meetings

What to Expect: Tutor Meetings

If you are lucky, you might have been able to meet your tutor before you started your placement. Not all universities allow time for this but if yours does, make sure you take the opportunity to introduce yourself and put a face to a name. It will calm your nerves when it comes to observations if you feel like you have built up a rapport with someone. Your tutor will most likely have some standard forms for you to fill in during your first meeting which is normally just before or after your first observation. Your tutor may ask you which particular areas you would like them to focus on when it comes to feedback. This could be one or more of the standards that you feel you need some extra help with. After each observation, you will discuss together targets for you to work on before your next observation.

Your tutor's role is to observe you and help you progress through the course. Some will be helpful and give you honest but constructive feedback, while others may not be quite as inspiring. In order to get off to a good start (and save time), you should come to all meetings prepared.

What to Prepare

- You will need to make sure you have all your paperwork up to date. Everything should be signed by the relevant parties and any observations that the school has completed should also be easily accessible.

- Try to prepare a few questions you would like to ask your tutor. It saves emailing them constantly with small queries.

- Make sure you also list any tasks you need your tutor to do, such as signing off documents or filling in forms. Give them as much notice as possible as no one likes to be rushed.

What If Your Tutor Is a Nightmare?

- We can't all get on and the fact that it is your tutor's role to offer (constructive) criticism may not help any uneasy feelings between the two of you. If you feel unhappy with your tutor, the first thing you should do is speak to them. Be polite but also don't be scared to say you feel you need more support.

There is an emphasis on the PGCE course that you should do things on your own, but this does not mean you are not entitled to support. Try to write a list of the areas you are struggling with and show how you have tried to solve them. This shows that you have tried and that you are not looking to be spoon fed.

- If this doesn't work, go to the university. You should have a course leader you can speak to. Don't make it personal by insulting the tutor or saying they aren't very good. You need to say that you feel you need some extra help (which you have discussed with your tutor) but you don't feel the support offered is quite what you were looking for. Again, go prepared with a list.

- Tutors come in many shapes and sizes and will have different supportive styles. During my placement, I experienced both ends of the scale. At the one end, I had a tutor who I felt expected me to know everything from day one which made me feel very unsupported. The feedback was fair and honest but lacked ways to improve my teaching which then left me pondering on how to improve. I would be a nervous wreck and regularly burst into tears of frustration. I even contemplated leaving the course. Some people do brilliantly under 'sink or swim' conditions; I was not one of those people. The other tutor I had was completely different. They were relaxed and not only provided feedback, but also ways in which to implement improvements. I regained my confidence and was able to start offering my own suggestions. Obviously, everyone has a preference for learning and the type of support they like, but if you are unhappy, don't wait until the end of the placement to say something.

- In the worst-case scenario, you need to remember that you will only deal with this person for a year (and only on a handful of occasions).

What to Expect: Mentor Meetings

Your mentor could be either your class teacher or someone else in the school, such as a senior leader. If your mentor is your class teacher, you will need to make a big effort to get on as this person is someone you will be spending a lot of time with.

You need to be as respectful as possible when your mentor is your class teacher as you are just a guest (so don't go making radical changes without first discussing them). Most won't mind you making small changes or trying out new things as long as you ask. Your mentor's role is to offer support and suggestions for improvement.

Do make sure you schedule a weekly or daily time to go over lesson plans. There is nothing worse than having someone ask to see your plans and then asking you to amend something half an hour before the lesson starts.

How to Prepare

- Don't half-arse things. Be overly prepared and be ready to answer questions about why you have decided to teach/ deliver a topic in a certain way.

- Mentors want to see that you are implementing their suggestions. One piece of praise I received from a mentor was, 'I make a suggestion and she just does it.' If I was given some feedback, I would make sure I included it in the next lesson I taught and in the next observation lesson. Even if I really didn't like it or didn't think it worked, I had at least showed that I had tried it. I learnt some really good techniques this way. Your mentor has to show you've progressed and one of the easiest ways to do that is to follow their feedback and start implementing it.

What If Your Mentor Is a Nightmare?

If your mentor is your class teacher, you will have to be careful in how you deal with the situation as they may take your comments to heart. For issues such as needing more support, speak to your mentor first. Tell them you are struggling in a particular area (e.g. lesson planning) and explain that you would appreciate a more experienced pair of hands to help. Arrange a time to suit you both to discuss the issue and make sure you come prepared with examples of what you have tried and where you struggle.

If the issue is of a more serious nature then ask your tutor or university to intervene on your behalf. Mediation can be suggested which might help or if it has become unbearable, a new class or school might be more appropriate. I spent the last few weeks of one placement dreading seeing my class teacher to the point where I contemplated leaving and not coming back. Don't let one person ruin your learning experience; seek outside help.

Being Observed and How to Prepare for It

Everyone, including experienced teachers, dislikes being observed. There is usually more planning involved, and you feel you are being judged and that the person watching you is trying to catch you out. Unfortunately, this is an important part of your development as both a trainee and qualified teacher so the best you can do is find ways to cope.

I was a complete wreck for my first placement when it came to observations. Parts of the lesson that I did without thinking were never written down in the plan and I also wouldn't put my plan down. Instead, I clutched it like a safety blanket (something I never did in unobserved lessons). I felt that even if I did something well, there would always be something I did badly.

It was only in my second placement that I rationalised things as follows:

1. I need to be more in-depth in my observed plans. I might use bullet points in my normal plans or not even mention certain things as I do them all the time, but my observer doesn't know that.

2. Think of observations like training wheels. You need more support and need to show you can plan in a more in-depth manner before you can do it on your own. It is only by seeing how you plan that mentors and tutors can offer support and help you to improve.

3. No lesson is perfect. Even if the lesson goes brilliantly, the observer will still pick up on something. They too need to show you are improving although it does sometimes feel like pointless feedback. I was once told that I had used the wrong colour paper for modelling writing a sentence. It seemed petty at the time but it meant when I was observed for the second time and I used white paper, I could show I had listened to feedback and improved.

4. One of the most important things I tried to remind myself was this: No. One. Died. It is only a lesson observation and you are not going to face the firing squad for one bad lesson. Find out what went wrong, take on board the feedback and make sure the next lesson is better. When you are caught up in such an

intense course, negatives can seem more out of proportion than they normally would be.

Once you realise these four simple things, you will relax. At the end of the day, a bad observation is not the worst thing in the world. If you have a good mentor, they will show you how to improve. The best mentor I had was able to break down feedback into small, achievable goals that could be easily addressed. Only once I had completed a few did she give me more. This was less daunting than having ten things suddenly thrown at me to improve for my next observation.

The more observations you do, the better you will become at them. See them for what they are, a way to measure progress but not a personal judgement, and you will be fine.

How to Prepare for Observations

The key to a good observation is preparation. Before you start, you should ask yourself the following questions:

- Have you been given a particular lesson to plan for?
  - o If this is your first observation and you haven't been given a specific subject, ask to teach a lesson in a subject you are confident in. You will be a bag of nerves if you are asked to teach PE lesson having never done so before.
  - o Once you have done your first observation, it will become easier. Don't make the mistake of trying to always pick your favourite subject to be observed in. How will you ever improve in subjects you are less confident at teaching if you are never given feedback for them?
- Have you got schemes of work?
  - o In order to plan an effective lesson, you will want to see what the children have done before and what they need to learn next. You need to be able to show that you can plan a lesson within a sequence as this is a skill you will need as a teacher. Always ask the class teacher if you need some extra help.
- Have you got time to prepare?
  - o Is it a morning or afternoon lesson?

o   It is important to allow yourself set-up time, especially if you have experiments or practical elements to your lesson.

o   Prepare as much as you can the night before. Check all equipment before the observation and have all work printed ready for the children. If you have worksheets, stick them in the books beforehand to save the children wasting time fighting over glue sticks.

Once you have decided the basics, you need to plan.

• Don't try something new if the children are not used to it. You don't want to spend valuable time explaining the rules for a new game.

• Your plan will most likely be more in-depth than usual and more explicit. Don't just say 'elicit feedback with questions', but instead list the questions you will ask.

• You will also want to show you've included students of all levels. One way to do this is to pick three children of 'high', 'middle' and 'low' ability. Use these children to gauge understanding. If you are still unsure, ask another child from the same ability group.

• You will also want to make sure your lesson objective is achievable and can be assessed.

Your head may be all over the place so here is a checklist to remind you what to do the day before and what to do on the day:

The day before - just before you leave school, ideally:

• Check any electrical/ supporting equipment works

• Check you have enough supplies (rulers, pencils etc.)

• Print all sheets and stick in books if needed

• Set up a chair for the observer

• Check the seating plan for the class- move any children that will fight/play up

• Make sure you are up to date with your marking in that subject

• Are there any last-minute changes to your lesson plan you need to make?

The day of the lesson observation:

- Check electrics
- Lay out supplies and set up experiment equipment
- Make sure you have a list of things to discuss with your tutor and have the correct paperwork ready

As long as you can honestly say you've prepared, you will be fine.

Planning

Planning will be a key part of your teaching career. You will spend a significant amount of time preparing new plans for your class.

Throughout your PGCE, you will see many examples of plans. Some experienced teachers may write a few sentences on a post-it note, while others will stick rigidly to their A4 page plan. While you are learning, don't worry if your plans run into several pages. Your university or school may have a set document for lesson planning and it's important that you follow their guidelines.

To save yourself time, use pre-existing lesson plans to gain ideas, or simply adapt them for your class. The following are just some examples of where to find lesson plans.

Where to Get Plans

School Systems

Some schools require you to upload plans before or after each lesson. Now, this sounds like a pain but, on the plus side, if you are covering the same topic this year then it gives you a good starting point. It is also a good way to familiarise yourself with the school's system of planning as each school will vary. It is always best to check first with your class teacher whether it is okay to use the plans and if they are still up to date. Do make sure you upload (if asked) your own plans so that others can use them too.

Other Teachers

You won't be able to rely on other teachers forever but, as a student, I would highly recommend seeking out subject specialists in the school to ask them for advice on planning and to see examples of excellent lessons. Most subject specialists will be keen to share their knowledge but be mindful that they are taking time out of their busy day to help. Always ask well in advance and be flexible about when you are able to meet.

The Internet

I hesitate to add this category as there are so many appalling websites trying to charge you money for poor plans. You need to be hyper-vigilant when it comes to using plans you find online and always ask other teachers for their recommendations in regard to good websites.

I knew several student teachers who did not want to use pre-made plans as they felt it was lazy. Each to their own I suppose. My view was that pre-made plans were a good crutch to start with as they are usually written by very experienced teachers who have perfected the art of lesson planning. You should always adapt any plan anyway (even those from the school's own system) to suit your class. Using pre-made plans gave me loads of new ideas to use in my teaching that I wouldn't have thought of otherwise.

Another great place to gain support and ideas is through Facebook groups. I joined one for primary MFL which I found very helpful as there were very experienced teachers willing to share ideas. You will find groups based on specific subjects, age phases and even year groups.

You will find a list of planning websites to help you at the back of this book.

How to Plan Quickly

It took me nearly until the end of my course to realise that the work produced at the end of the lesson was not the most important thing when it came to lesson planning. Sure, a lovely picture or poster about the lifecycle of a plant was nice, but did it really show what the child had learnt that lesson?

The basics of a lesson are:

- A learning intention/aim
    - o   This is what the children will be able to do by the end of the lesson
    - o   E.g. Aim: I can describe how to plant a sunflower seed.
- The success criteria
    - o   This is how you will assess how well the child has achieved the aim, usually by using "I can" statements.
    - o   E.g.:
        - ▪   All: I can plant a sunflower seed

- Most: I can write instructions on how to plant a sunflower seed
- Some: I can think of questions to ask about plants that I would like to know.

- Keywords:
  o New words the children will need to understand to complete the task.
    - Seeds, soil, water and plants.
- Resources and equipment:
  o Anything you need for the lesson
    - Soil, pots, water and seeds.
- Starter
  o This is a warm-up for the first part of the lesson. One way to start if this is your first lesson with a new class is to ask the children what they know already about the topic.
  o If it is part of a series of lessons, you can ask the children to recap what they did last time.
    - E.g. With your partner, list three things you remember learning from the last lesson.
  o If you are using equipment, you might also introduce the equipment to the children and ask them to discuss the uses of each item with their partner.
- Main
  o This is the main part of the lesson. It is how you will achieve the aim. It is important to model any written work and practical work before you expect the children to do it on their own. If more than one thing needs to be done, break down the task into smaller parts and model how it should be done.
  o E.g. Show the children how to plant the seeds in the soil, add water and label them. Ask them to talk you through each stage.
  o Then on the whiteboard, model the instructions. Ask which step came first (to up-level this, encourage the use of descriptive words).
  o Choose three children to clarify what you have to do (high, middle and lower ability).

- o Ask if anyone needs help. If so, keep them on the carpet.
- o Send children to their tables (one group at a time).
- o Walk around and help, or sit with one table.
- o Extension: children write questions about plants that they would like to know the answers to. See if their partner knows the answer. If you have enough tablets, children could research the answer and report back to their partner.
- Plenary
  - o This is where you combine all the knowledge the children have learnt that lesson.
    - ▪ Eg. Ask children to share with their partner what they have leant today.
  - o Games can also be used or a large match game (match words to pictures as class/tables).
  - o If you have a KWL chart, you can add to the 'L' (what we've learnt) section to move on learning.

Once you understand how to get the bare bones planned (as above) you can start to flesh it out. Some mentors like to see everything you will do (including the questions you will ask) while others some don't mind a scaled down version.

I used to find doing the above as a mind map would sometimes help with planning. Make sure you know what the aim of the whole scheme is; there is no point in doing a lesson on planting seeds if it isn't going to help learning later on.

Troubleshooting

- Lessons are dull:
  - o Not every lesson will be exciting, but that doesn't mean you can't try. Can you add a practical element? Have you looked at other teachers' ideas? Can you use a game or video as a starter to hook the class?
- Lessons are too short:
  - o In an effort to slim down, sometimes we cut too much or underestimate how quickly children can complete the work. Is the work challenging enough for the group?

Can you add meaningful extensions? Can you have more talking partner activities?

- Lessons are too long:
  - n The opposite problem can also occur with lessons which are too long. Are all activities meaningful? Will they help to progress learning? What can you remove from your lesson and still achieve the learning intention/aim?

- Not enough differentiation:
  - o The easiest and most effective way I have seen differentiation work is the 'All, Most and Some' method. This works with the idea that the children are not limited by ability but can choose how far they want to push themselves.
  - o Strip the topic to basics: what is the minimum needed to achieve the learning objective? This is your 'All'.
  - o What could the children do on top of that to up-level their work or push themselves? This is your 'Most'.
  - o Your higher ability children should be stretched by the 'Some' objective and they should be encouraged to achieve this level.

During my placements, I was given the advice that I should always have a high, middle and lower ability child in mind when planning my lessons. I would then make sure I asked these children questions during the lesson to make sure they understood what was required. Change which children you think of each lesson. It might also help to look through each of the three children's books to see how they are coping with the current work. I found this very helpful.

Reflections

Whether you like it or not, reflection is a skill you are going to have to master as a teacher.

When you have your own class, your reflection will not be as formal, but it will still happen. In my first placement, I tended to rush my reflections on a Sunday night, ready to be signed off on Monday. I spent no effort on them and it showed. I thought it was pointless and I think, in hindsight, that my lack of effort in regard to reflection contributed to my lack of success in that placement.

For my second placement, I made it a personal aim to jot down notes after each lesson (and sometimes during) that I could reflect on after school. Once I started doing this, I noticed my practice improved markedly as I started noticing things I hadn't before.

Depending on your placement, you may or may not have formal reflection paperwork to complete. If you do, follow your university's guidelines. If you don't, I would still recommend doing your own informal form of reflection. Some questions you could ask might include:

- What went well? Why?
- What could have been improved? Why?
- If you taught this lesson again, what would you change?
- Did you try a new technique? Did it go well?

These few questions should set you off thinking about your practice and what needs to be improved.

Running the Class

In your first placement, you will probably feel like an intruder. The class teacher will teach most of the lessons, with you jumping in occasionally. This can be hard for you as a trainee to develop your own style, but it is a brilliant time to learn what does and does not suit your teaching ethos. I spent a significant amount of time in my first placement observing and researching methods to try out in my second teaching experience.

Setting a Routine

While you will need to discuss any new routines with the class teacher, setting your own routines will show the children what to expect from you. Never go behind the class teacher's back and do sometimes without asking first. It is their class after all.

To start, it is best to follow the class teacher's routine exactly. The children will know you are an outsider but by showing them you know the rules, it's less likely that they will push you. I made the frequent mistake of asking the children questions about playtimes and routines which made it painfully obvious that I was new.

Gather ideas from your class teacher and also take the chance to watch others. You can learn a lot by watching other teachers. Researching ideas to try from forums or academic sources is also something I would try to make time for. It will help your practice in the long run.

Behaviour Management

Much like routines, you will need to ask your class teacher before you change anything. You will also need to be mindful of the school's own behaviour policy. How you handle behaviour management will be a very personal thing. One piece of advice I would give is to expose yourself to as many different viewpoints as you can: attend lectures, read articles or books and observe other teachers. Build up an arsenal of ideas that can be used in a variety of situations and with different classes; what works for one class won't work for another.

A few pieces of advice I gained from my placements:

- Reward good behaviour. Some schools operate a 'catch me when I am good' system where you praise excellent behaviour rather than focusing on the bad. It can be as simple as 'well done for writing within the lines.' Make it specific to the child rather than a generic comment which will have less impact. I found this worked very well for chatty children. If a table was a little noisy, I would praise a child who was working quietly on that table. I would then make a conscious effort to catch the chatty children working quietly and praise them too. Not all children will care about being praised, but this is a better first strategy than jumping into punishments immediately.

- Use positive language first. No one likes being told off and some children can instantly switch off if they feel like they are being moaned at. Much like the above advice, don't focus on the negative behaviour first. If you notice a child talking or messing about, sit next to them and ask them how they are getting on. Get them to explain what they have done so far and find out if they are struggling with anything. Find something to meaningfully praise. I always liked to say something like, 'it is so lovely to see how hard you've worked today, keep it up' or 'you've worked really well today. I'm looking forward to seeing what else you've done at the end of the lesson' before moving on. If you have time, do try to go back and comment on what they've done since you left. Not only will the child know that you will be expecting something, but they will also appreciate the praise. This is far less aggressive than instantly starting with staying in during break.

- Silent treatment. If the whole class or the majority are messing around then this technique can work well. I rarely shouted at my class as a teacher as I didn't feel it was a good use of my voice. I was also given the advice that the children know as soon as you shout that you've lost control. If the class is loud, start by asking them firmly but politely to quieten down as it is too loud. If the class doesn't, write a '1' on the board. This is the amount of time they will be kept in over break. Keep adding more time every 30 seconds until the class quietens down. When they are quiet and focused, explain to them that the time on the board is how many minutes they will be staying behind during break. Always give children the chance to earn the time back. If you still have a few refusing to work well, draw a sad face on the board, write their names underneath and add time individually (which also can be earnt off). The most time I ever added was seven minutes. After a few days of having the children stay in, I would only have to ask for the class to quieten down as I walked to the board and there would be silence.

- Get to their level. Whenever you are talking to a child, make sure you get to their level by either sitting down or kneeling. Being small and having an adult tower over you can be intimidating. Always give the child your full attention and don't interrupt them either. Respect works both ways.

- Build a bond. One thing I really noticed when teaching was the link between how you deal with children and their attitude to their work. I found the children produced their best work when they felt I liked them and was interested. Now, I am not advocating being their best friend, but try to show an interest in each child. I would always make sure I talked to everyone as they hung up their coats. It took a while for them to be comfortable with me but you soon find out a lot about each child as an individual.

- Show and tell. Both of my placement classes were very chatty. If you gave them any chance to do so, they would talk, mostly about what they did over the weekend or their plans for after school. I was struggling to think of potential outlets for the children while still maintaining order during the lesson. I did some research and found some teachers used 'show and tell' at the end of the day to allow the children to tell the class any news. I found this very helpful when the class was too chatty as I could say 'we won't have time for show and tell if we don't finish our work'. The chatty children had an outlet at the end of the day and felt they were being listened to, but during a scheduled time. I also extended this by encouraging the children to bring in a book that we could read as a class. Even the children that hated reading would bring in a book to share. This did backfire once when a child forgot their book and gave me a dictionary from the back of the class, but I had a lot of fun making up a story while pretending to read it to five-year-olds.

What to Do When You Leave

Hopefully, you've had such a wonderful time at your placement school that you are going to be sad when you leave. It is best to make a good final impression as you may need a reference. So, even if you had an awful time, make sure you make an effort even if it's just for the children's sake.

I would ask your class teacher if you could do something fun for your last day; a film or an experiment might be nice. I brought in a film and gave the children popcorn when I left one placement. Always ask before you bring in food as some schools don't like it.

A card to your class teacher (as well as some chocolates) will always be appreciated. A card to the whole class is also a nice touch. I would also get a card for your mentor to say thank you for their help.

Before you leave, make sure you take everything with you as your class teacher will not want to hold on to your things if you forget them. Also, make sure you return all resources to the correct place or person.

Finally, if the placement went really well, I would ask your mentor if you could use them as a reference after you leave. Keep these details safe as you won't want to be chasing someone when you need a reference later on.

6
QTS Folder

'Education is the key to success in life, and teachers make a lasting impact in the lives of their students.'

Solomon Ortiz

University Evidence

Depending on your placements, you may have a few weeks in university. During the first university period, your aim is to have one piece of evidence for each standard. If you then do a second placement at university, you will also want to gain a second piece of evidence for each standard too. When you come to handing in your folder, unless told otherwise by your university, you will only need one piece per standard based on your university experience. It's better to start with two and filter it down than have none and have to scramble around at the end of the course. Put all this evidence in your QTS folder (ideally using dividers for each standard).

When gathering evidence, it is worth writing which standard the evidence relates to on the top of each piece of evidence. Although it is best to use different examples for each standard (for variety), you can use a piece for more than one standard. If you have a piece of evidence that you think would be good for two standards, choose the strongest one and then add the other standard number next to it. This will allow the person looking at your folder to see that you have thought about the standard and have extra evidence.

My university also recommended adding a post-it note to explain in a few lines why this was the best evidence for this standard.

Examples for the standards for university (numbers correspond to the standard numbers):

1. Mini-lesson plans, SEN provisions and equal opportunity notes.
2. Examples of higher order questions, short/medium/long time plans, assessment for learning examples, notes on theories of progress/outcomes and use of data.
3. Assessment phase sheets, subject knowledge notes and notes on subject lectures.
4. Mini-lesson plans showing that you have thought about planning (starter, main and plenary).
5. Showing how you use differentiation, provisions for EAL learners and notes on diversity.

6. Notes on assessments and feedback in mini-lessons.

7. Lecture notes, mini-lessons and feedback, as well as own research on topics.

8. Risk assessments and own research on particular issues to do with teaching.

9. (Part two): Safeguarding notes, attendance records and lecture notes showing that you have thought about how you can plan sensitively.

Any evidence you use that contains personal information about children must be edited. You can either blank out names or use initials or first names. Use common sense; obviously, if you are writing about your experience in a Year Three class at Random Primary School and are talking about a child called Sadie Smith, it might be best to use just an initial.

Schedule an hour at the end of each block of university or placement time to go through and gather two pieces of evidence for each standard. You can filter it down to your final pieces at the end.

School Experience Evidence

As with your university evidence, you will need two pieces of evidence for each standard, for each placement (so four in total: two for SE1 and two for SE2). You can sort these out later in the year.

Examples for the standards for placements (numbers correspond to the standard numbers):

1. Lesson plans- SEN, differentiation, observation notes and reflections.

2. Reflections on lessons, examples of higher order questions/ extension work, reflective notes and showing improvement via data.

3. Self-assessment and mentor notes detailing subject knowledge, schemes of work, own research into using literacy and numeracy across the curriculum.

4. Observations, lesson plans (starter, main and plenary), medium and long-term plans.

5. Differentiation of resources, focus studies on SEN pupils, observation notes and reflection work.

6. Showing you have used data in planning by revisiting weaker areas of understanding and showing you are acting on feedback.

7. Observations, research notes, reflections and seating plans, as well as plans for use of support staff.

8. Using support staff, risk assessments, planning with others, notes from mentor, notes from meetings and running a club.

9. (Part two) Attending meetings (notes), running assemblies and mentor notes.

Once you have finished your placement, you should sort your files. Choose two pieces of evidence for each standard for SE1 and two pieces of evidence for each standard for SE2. Do this at the end of each placement to save time.

Remember, you can also use any directed activities that directly relate to these standards in your folder too. Just don't rely on them as your only source of evidence.

Enrichment Evidence

if your university does offer an enrichment placement, you will need to find extra evidence. My enrichment placement was only two weeks, but I still collected a large amount of evidence due to having quite a few directed activities.

Examples for the standards for enrichment (numbers correspond to the standard numbers):

1. How to differentiate lessons
2. Research or advice about a SEN child
3. MFL/computing Planning (or other specialisms you may take)
4. How your school teaches ICT/notes on ways to teach it
5. Notes on learning types
6. How schools use assessment and research notes
7. Behaviour management strategies
8. Communication with parents
9. (Part Two) British values- how does the school tackle this? Assemblies, lessons or discussions are some examples.

As with the university and placement ideas, make sure you keep two pieces of evidence for each standard.

End of the Course

When you start your PGCE, you will most likely be told when your file is due. If you use the Excel spreadsheet provided or a diary, make sure that this date is written down. You will probably still be on your last placement when your folder is due in and teaching an 80% timetable (and all the planning that goes with it!) so time is precious.

If you have followed the advice above, you should now have two pieces of evidence for each standard: two for university (or possibly four if you have two large blocks); two for SE1; two for SE2; and two for enrichment. You now need to filter this down. Look at each standard (and the notes on your post-it notes) and see which of the two for each section best show that you understand and have met the standard.

If you have evidence that can be used for more than one standard, it's best (rather than using the same information twice) to choose where it is stronger and use if for that standard. An example would be having notes on behaviour management (standard 7) but also, on the same page, having notes on how to adapt your teaching style (standard 5). If I felt this evidence was better placed in standard 7, I might also highlight the part that could be used for standard 5 and write the number five at the top of the page (in brackets, after the seven, saying something like: 'can also be used for standard...').

The aim of your QTS folder is to prove to the invigilator that you should pass the course. Plans will most likely be your main source of evidence, as well as mentor notes. As long as you have a good variety of supporting evidence, you will be fine.

7
Finishing

'Learning is not attained by chance, it must be sought for with ardor and diligence.'

Abigail Adams

For this chapter, you will need to spend time going through your folder in order to make sure you have everything ready for submission. Don't skimp on this stage. Trust me, it will only make your life ten times harder when you have to fill in missing pages or scrabble around for extra evidence.

QTS Folder

- If you are lucky, your university will provide you with a rough outline of what they expect to see in your folder.

- At my university, we had a cover sheet showing how we had to lay out our PDP file. It was broken up into five sections, and listed a series of pieces of evidence that had to be in each section.

- Near the end of my last placement, I started organising my folder by purchasing some dividers (five).

- I would only put something in my folder if the evidence and post-it note was complete (see Chapter Six)

- I would recommend writing down the order in which you have filed evidence (if this is not provided for you). If you drop your file or it goes missing, you need to make sure you can sort it quickly. An example would be:

  o Standard 3/4: a lesson plan that shows good curriculum knowledge and how to plan and teach a well-structured lesson.

  o I have included this plan as I focused on literacy (cross-curriculum). I have also taken into account the previous knowledge the students had by looking at the previous lessons taught in this subject.

Tick List- What Needs to Be Done

- Do you need to get your tutor to sign anything? Not all evidence needs to be in the folder.

- Have you passed and included all subject audits (maths, English and science)?

- Have you included your assignment scores?

- Have you completed all directed activities and had them signed off?

- Have you included all evidence for the standards (at least two for each one)?

- Have you had all your Assessment Phase sheets signed off?

- Have you completed your Induction Year Profile and has it been sent to the correct people?

- If you have already secured a job, do you need to let your university know the contact details?

- Do you need to complete anymore evaluations?

- Is there anything else you haven't done that needs to be done before you can hand in your PDP?

Induction Profile

- What Is It?

  o Your Induction Profile is a document to help support you in your NQT year.

  o It is a bit like a CV but with details of targets you want to achieve. Your profile also acts as a way to introduce yourself to your new school, as well as show the school which areas you feel you need help in.

  o Your training provider should let you know how to layout your document but it is best to have a few details to hand. These include:

    ▪ Your contact details

    ▪ Your training provider, phase and training route

    ▪ Details of your new school and assigned mentor (if known)

    ▪ Previous placements (include contact details if you have permission)

    ▪ Make sure you include any extra tasks you helped with (such as running a club) and areas of the curriculum you taught. You don't need to go into a great deal of detail.

  o You may also be asked to add a reflection section to your document. This section will ask you about your strengths, what you found most fulfilling about your training year, and where you feel you would benefit from extra support.

  o You won't be required to write an essay for each question; a paragraph for each section should suffice. Be honest and clear in your answers; this document is designed to help you.

  o Finally, you will be expected to set key targets for yourself to complete in your induction year. My university requested a minimum of three targets but this can differ depending on your institution. It is better to have three SMART (specific, measurable, achievable, realistic and time based) targets than five vague ones. It goes without saying that your targets should be linked to the teaching standards. As an example, my three targets were as follows:

- S4- I would like to stick to timings I set out in lesson plans so that the children have a chance to finish their work. This may include changing my lesson plans to include only the most essential elements.

- S4- I would like to work on adjusting wait times when I ask questions to the class. I can reduce this by having the children discuss their idea with their talking partner first.

- S1- I would like to allow the children more of a role in the lesson so that I am a facilitator rather than a lecturer. I can achieve this by observing more experienced teachers to see how I can adapt my teaching style to allow the children to take on a more active role.

o Your aim is to show by the end of your NQT year that you have attempted to work towards these targets. It is very important to be realistic: there is no reason to set yourself up to fail by expecting all your lessons to be outstanding.

o Make sure you have sent the document to the correct person and you place a copy in your PDP if required.

Troubleshooting

- You have failed your last placement or are set to fail your last placement

  o Firstly, you need to find out why you are failing. Is it one specific issue or several? If there were longstanding issues, you should have been made aware of these long before the end of your placement so you could correct them. The best way to do this is to book a meeting with your tutor and mentor, either together or separately, and find out what you need to do to pass. If there are serious concerns, you may have the opportunity to re-sit this placement at another school.

  o During my training, I missed a few days due to sickness and had to make these up at the end of the last placement. Most training providers will build in a grace period to allow you to make up extra days.

  o Make sure you take detailed notes about what you need to do. Try and leave the meeting with some SMART targets that you can work on over an agreed period of time. It is also wise to book a follow up appointment with either your tutor or mentor to check your progress.

  o If there are serious issues or you don't feel that you are completely at fault, then I would suggest asking to see the Head of Course (or similar title). They are the person in charge of the PGCE and can help you to get back on track.

- You haven't managed to secure a job at the end of your PGCE

  o This isn't a huge issue. If you live in a large city or town, you will see jobs advertised fairly regularly around 'end of term' time as this is when people have to give notice if they want to leave the following term. It is best to wait for the right school rather than rush.

  o You can complete work via an agency for up to five years before needing to complete your NQT year. You can also do your NQT year as a supply teacher but you must spend a term (minimum) in the same school for it to count.

  o Personally, I would wait for a full-time, permanent position. If you fail your NQT year, you can no longer teach in state schools. You can, however, still teach in independent schools. You can appeal and add an extension to your NQT year but it would have to be under exceptional circumstances.

- You don't want to do your NQT year

  o There is no shame in deciding you do not want to be a teacher anymore. Many people realise that they just can't continue with the long hours and stress of a modern classroom. The fact that you got this far is excellent.

  o While you may not use lesson plans in an office job, the ability to plan in advance and deliver on time is a desirable skill many employers are looking for.

  o If you type 'careers instead of teaching' into a search engine, you will find plenty of people in the same situation.

  o I would say that it is still worth completing your induction profile and any extra paperwork in case you do decide to go back into teaching at a later date. A term or even a year out might make you miss the classroom.

  o At the end of the day, you need to do what is best for you. Deciding you do not like something after having a go at it does not make you a failure. Teaching is not an easy career by any means and I would urge anyone who doesn't feel it's for them to pursue something else. Do what makes YOU happy.

8
Applying for Jobs

'Education is the best provision for old age.'

Aristotle

Applications, Not CVs

I have yet to meet a school that requires a CV over their own application form, even for a TA role.

Most forms will requiro you to list your work history over a set period of time (say, the last ten years) or your whole career. For this reason, it is always best to keep track of everything in a Word document or Excel spreadsheet. You will need to include:

- Dates you started and finished work
- Job title
- Main duties
- Reference details
- Training and certificates you gained while employed

Even if the job isn't related to teaching, it is best to include all jobs as some employers will require your full work history for child protection reasons. Having everything to hand also makes your life a whole lot easier as everything is easy to find.

As part of my course, we had to produce a CV. While we couldn't submit it to a school, the idea was to write down our work history and create a personal statement which would help us when it came to filling in applications.

You will only need to include relevant jobs on a CV, not all of them. It is worth keeping a hard copy and a virtual copy to hand in case you come across a job with a short deadline and you want to send an application quickly. A basic CV will include the following:

- Personal details
- Education
- Teaching experience
- Other relevant experience
- Interests/hobbies
- Additional skills
- Referees

Cover Letters

Regardless of whether you send your application via snail mail or email, you will need to include a cover letter (unless specified not to). This is a brief letter that points the reader to your skills without having to read through your entire application form.

There are a plethora of templates on the internet to help you draft a covering letter but the bare minimum you should include is as follows:

- A short introduction explaining who you are
- Why you would suit the role
- What you can bring to the job (think professional skills, soft skills and your interests)
- A final few sentences in which you should add: a thank you to the reader, a request that they get in touch if further information is required, and a sign off indicating that you hope to hear from them soon.

Personal Statements

While you can have a generic personal statement ready for any job you apply for, it is best to be specific and personalise the statement to suit the role. You will be using your statement to show off your skills and why you are the best person for the job. You will need to include the following paragraphs:

- Paragraph 1: Refer to the job you are applying for and why you are applying.

   o Show you have done your research about the school and have attended visits. If the school has a particular focus, such as improving literacy (which is a particular strength of yours), now is the time to show off in this paragraph. This is no time to be modest!

- Paragraph 2: Details about your PGCE.

   o Did you specialise in a topic? Would this be of use to the school? Mention your degree – are there any relevant modules you can link to the post you are applying for?

- Paragraph 3: Mention your teaching experience.

   o If the post is for a particular age range, then make sure you include that you have experience of that age range. Mention successes you have had and examples that show off your differentiation or brilliant behaviour management skills. If you don't have experience in this age range, you will need to show how you can meet the demands of this age range. You will want to show adaptability.

- Paragraph 4: Your views on teaching.

   o How does your philosophy fit in with the ethos of the school? What has informed your views and why? If you hold similar beliefs to the school, draw attention to this with examples of how you transfer these views into your teaching.

- Paragraph 5: Extra skills.

   o Do you teach music lessons or have an interest in painting? Mention it. Schools are always looking for extra people to help out at events or to run clubs. Show them you are more than just a teacher. You are the complete package.

- Paragraph 6: The last paragraph

  o   Finish with a positive statement indicating how you feel you would fit in at the school and that you believe your experience makes you an excellent candidate for the role.

Once you have an outline, you can easily adapt this statement for each role.

Prospective Letters

If you have not managed to secure a job by the end of the course, you can consider sending a prospective letter to a few local headteachers. Much like a personal statement, you are showing off your skills to potential schools in the hopes that you will be considered should a job become available. If you have a CV, you can send it along with this letter although, should a job come up, you may be required to fill in an application form too.

An example of a few paragraphs to include are:

- Paragraph 1: Mention your current situation.
  - o Are you currently still on your PGCE or have you finished? Explain that you feel that you would like to work at the school and give a reason why. Mention that it is because you want to work at the school that you have decided to send a letter just in case a vacancy were to arise.
- Paragraph 2: Research.
  - o Mention research you have undertaken about the school, e.g. through its website or its OFSTED report. Show you have taken the time to research the school and that you are interested in what they offer.
- Paragraph 3: Your skills.
  - o Draw attention to your skills and how they could benefit the school. Are they focusing on improving a particular department? Will your skills help them to achieve this?
- Paragraph 4: Your experience and ethos.
  - o Show how your experience and ethos would suit the school. Give a brief example of both to demonstrate this.
- Paragraph 5: A final statement
  - o A final statement about you and your interests. Show you have extra skills that could be used.
- Paragraph 6: Thank you.
  - o Thank the person for reading and mention that you would be happy to explain further in person any details included in your CV or personal statement.

How to Prepare for Interviews

Congratulations on getting an interview!

This means that the school is interested in you and your skill set, so now is the time to prepare to show off. You don't want to be pushy, but you want to show that you are the best person for the job.

If you are invited to see the school before your interview, go! If you aren't, ask if it is possible to have a look around. Try and visit the staff room if you can to say hello. You want to show that you are a team player and could fit in.

A typical interview will be made up of a panel of interviewers, typically the Headteacher, the Deputy, and one or two governors. You will be asked to teach a sample lesson or do a presentation on a chosen subject (such as behaviour management).

You should make sure you ask questions if you are unsure and to show engagement. You need to know the age range and ability of the class you are going to teach. You will also need to know if there are any SEN children, as well as if there are any technical requirements. Try to avoid a lesson that is heavily reliant on technology as things will inevitably go wrong. Make sure you have a backup idea should the computer not be working.

In the interview, you will be asked questions to find out if you would be a good fit for the school. The panel may ask about your educational ethos or why you want to work at the school.

A few examples of questions you may be asked are:

- What else can you offer the school?
- Can you share an example of positive behaviour management you have used?
- Why do you want to teach this age range?
- What experience do you have of this age range?
- How would you deal with 'insert behaviour issue'?
- What support do you feel you would need from the school?

A question that threw me was when I was asked what my classroom would look like. I thought they wanted me to describe the decorating style but the panel were actually focusing on how I pictured the children in my classroom. For example, was my classroom silent or noisy? Were the children engaged? There are loads of interesting ways to answer this question and others discussed online. It is worth having an idea of the type of questions you will be asked and how you to answer them. Whatever questions you get asked, just make sure you have an example or two to show how you put your knowledge into practice.

On the day, make sure you are dressed presentably. A two-piece suit with a clean shirt will make you look professional. It is best to avoid looking too flamboyant or too informal as you want to make a good first impression. Make sure you pack everything you need to take with you the night before and put it next to your clothes so it doesn't get forgotten. I put a copy of my lesson plan on to a USB stick just in case something went wrong. I also bought my own whiteboard pen. Look over your application one more time to make sure you are familiar with what you wrote and you are confident enough to give great answers.

Interview Tips:

- Find out how long the lesson needs to be. Most will be quite short (20 minutes) and in that time you need a starter, main and plenary of some description. The interests of the class can be a great help but make sure your lesson is aimed at the right age range.
- Ask questions about the class. It shows engagement and interest.
- Limit your resources and have a backup for ICT.
- Make sure you build in time for the children to ask questions. You also want to make sure you ask them questions to check their understanding.
- Make sure your plan is highly detailed. The panel has never seen you before and you want to make sure they know you are doing certain things for a reason. So, write down your reasoning (briefly).

As hard as it is, do try to relax. The worst that can happen is that you don't get the job. And if that's the case, then they weren't the right school for you.

9
Appendix

'Education is the key to success in life, and teachers make a lasting impact in the lives of their students.'

Solomon Ortiz

All of the items listed below can also be downloaded and then edited from the resources area at: https://survivingyourpgce.com/category/resources/

Draft Work Experience Letter

Your name
The first line of your address
Your town/city
Your postcode
Your phone numbers
Your email addresses

Date

Name of person to address (normally the Headteacher)
Name of school
First line of address
Town or city
Postcode

RE: Work Experience Placement

Dear Sir/ Madam,

I am writing to you to enquire about the possibility of completing a (how many days? /weeks?) work experience placement at your school.

My name is .... and I am currently studying .... in the hope of becoming a primary school teacher. I am aware that as part of the application process, I need to gain experience in a primary school setting and I would love to have the opportunity to gain this experience in your school. (You can write why you chose this school if you wish- did you go here as a child and have good memories? 'I would like to gain experience in your school because...')

I have had experience in .... (list experience – 'I have had experience in a Year One classroom/babysat/ran a football club and also have a younger brother so I am comfortable working with a variety of ages').

I am (list personal skills- friendly, reliable, approachable etc.). My personal interests are (reading/ learning a new language/playing an instrument / playing football etc.).

I am interested in working with children aged ... to .... as I (insert reason- e.g. 'have little experience in this age range and so would like to gain a broader overview of all age ranges)

or

I am interested in working with all children and I would be pleased to work with any age range that can accommodate me for my placement.

Preferences: Unless there is a specific reason why you would like a certain age range (e.g. have no experience so would like to gain some), it is best not to state a preference this early on as the school could struggle to find somewhere to put you. If you are asked at a later date, you can say 'I'd love to work in x age range as I (insert reason) but I am happy to go wherever you can place me.'

Thank you for taking the time to read this letter and I look forward to hearing from you.

Yours sincerely   if you know the name of the person you whom you are writing

Or

Yours faithfully   if you don't know the name of the person to whom you are writing (Dear Sir or Dear Madam).

Your signature:

Your name (printed)

Grey: Change/delete before sending.

PGCE Statement Planner

Below I have included a table to help you fill in the relevant sections. You should aim to try and include three examples for each. This will then help you during your interview.

Reasons why I want to be a teacher.			
Example to show you understand the challenges.			
Example to show you understand the rewards.			
Examples of how education has impacted on and benefited you.			
Examples of extra work experience and how it is relevant.			
Examples of extra curriculum activities that can benefit teaching.			

Okay, once you have the bare bones of your statement, you'll need to add some meat to it. Use the gaps below to turn the bullet points above into small paragraphs.

Introduction:

Reason for wanting to be a teacher:

Examples to show you understand that teaching is both rewarding and challenging:

Education and how it has had an impact on you:

Extra work experience:

Any skills you can bring to the teaching profession:

Conclusion:

Budget Plan

Whether you like budgeting or not, having a rough guide to how to spend your money will make your life easier. You will have a lot to worry about during your PGCE; don't let money be another thing to add to the list. You can make your budget easy and simple or break things down into complex categories; use whatever system you think is best for you. I've tried to do a simple budget below to get you started. An Excel version is also available on the website.

Income:
- Grants/loans:
- Work:
- Savings:
- Parents/relatives:
- Scholarships:
- Misc.:

Outgoings:
- Rent:
- Electric:
- Gas:
- Internet and landline:
- Mobile phone:
- Water:
- Council tax:
- Food:
- Socialising:
- University books:
- Printing:
- Special occasions:
- Transport:
- Clothing:
- Toiletries and grooming:
- Eating out/coffee etc:
- Medical:
- Misc/ emergency fund:

Quick Meal Ideas

The last thing you will want to do after coming back from a long day teaching is to spend ages cooking. You'll either make something unhealthy just because it's quick or end up trying to survive on a diet of fast food. Not only is this financially ruinous, but you can't be at your best living off junk.

I have included some quick meals as well as meals that take a little longer but can be frozen so will save you time in the long run. Most can have the portions doubled which means you will have some left over for lunch or dinner the next day.

You don't need any special equipment, but I would recommend buying:

- A frying pan
- A saucepan
- Sharp knives
- Grater
- Wooden spoon
- Potato masher
- Tin opener
- Chopping board
- Measuring jug
- Baking tray
- Ovenproof dish

Chicken and Bacon Pasta- 30 minutes. Serves 1.

A very basic, bog-standard pasta meal.

- Ingredients:
    - o 1 chicken breast, 2 slices of smoked or unsmoked bacon, 75g of pasta, 1 tin of chopped tomatoes, 1 teaspoon of dried basil, 1 tablespoon of oil, ½ teaspoon of garlic puree, ½ mug of peas, 1 pepper and a small amount of grated cheese.

- Method
  - o Put the pasta in a pan of boiling water and put on the hob. Occasionally stir to stop it sticking.
  - o Fry the chicken in a frying pan. Once it is cooked, add the bacon. Chop the pepper while you are waiting.
  - o Add the chopped tomatoes, basil, garlic, peas and pepper to the frying pan. Let all the ingredients simmer while the pasta is cooking.
  - o Once the pasta has cooked, add all the ingredients together and serve with some grated cheese on the top.

Pork Curry- 10 minutes. Serves 1.

Not the most imaginative meal but this was a stable of my diet as it is so versatile. I would always try to add 2/3 different types of vegetables to this meal to make sure I got as close to my five-a-day as possible. You can experiment with different meats and sauces.

- Ingredients:
  - o 75-100g of pork, ½ tin of curry sauce, variety of vegetables (carrots, peas, sweetcorn, mushrooms or peppers), 1 tablespoon of oil, microwave rice and poppadoms or naans.
- Method
  - o If using frozen vegetables, defrost in the microwave before cooking. This usually takes about five minutes depending on what vegetables you use.
  - o Fry the pork in oil in a frying pan until cooked. Once cooked, add the vegetables to the pan to heat up.
  - o Add the curry sauce and put the rice in the microwave.
  - o Serve in a bowl or plate with the rice, poppadoms or naans.

Prawn Pasta With Soft Cheese- 10 minutes. Serves 1

Another super easy meal but this time slightly more indulgent with the soft cheese.

- Ingredients
  - o Handful of frozen prawns, 75g spaghetti, three

tablespoons of soft cheese, such as Philadelphia (garlic and herb flavour), ½ mug of peas and mushrooms and 1 tablespoon of oil.

- Method
  o   Put the spaghetti on to cook in the boiling water.
  o   If using frozen vegetables, defrost in the microwave. The prawns need to be defrosted in warm water for around 20 minutes.
  o   Once the prawns are deforested, add to a frying pan with oil and fry.
  o   Add the vegetables to the pan.
  o   Once the vegetables are cooked, check the pasta. If it is cooked, drain it and dish up.
  o   Put the soft cheese in the pan on a low heat with the prawns and vegetables and stir for 1 minute until hot.
  o   Pour over the spaghetti and serve.

Casserole-2 hours. Serves 1.

The joy of a casserole is that you can chuck anything in it. I use this chicken version the most, but feel free to use what you already have.

- Ingredients
  o   2 chicken breasts, 4 slices of bacon, 1 carrot, 1 onion, 1 teaspoon of rosemary, 1 teaspoon of thyme, 1 leek, 1 teaspoon of garlic puree, 2 potatoes, 250ml of chicken stock (can use cubes) and 1 tablespoon of oil.
- Method
  o   Fry the chicken in a pan until brown on the outside.
  o   Add bacon to the pan and cook.
  o   While the meat is cooking, roughly chop all the vegetables.
  o   Make the stock (see instructions on packet).
  o   Once the meat is cooked, add the vegetables and cook for 5 minutes.
  o   Add the contents of the saucepan to a casserole dish and add all the herbs and garlic.

o   Put into a preheated oven at 180 degrees (fan) or 200 degrees for 30-45 minutes or until the veg is soft.

Deconstructed Cottage Pie- 30 minutes. Serves 4.

This recipe is for 4 portions. Freeze leftovers or use for dinner the next day to save time.

- Ingredients
    - o   6 medium potatoes, 500g of minced beef, 1 mug of peas, 1 mug of carrots, 1 onion, 1 tablespoon of butter, a splash of milk, 1 teaspoon of cornflour, 300ml of beef stock and 4 mushrooms.
- Method
    - o   Peel and chop the potatoes into four. Place into boiling water on the hob and simmer for 20 minutes.
    - o   Chop the vegetables and place to one side.
    - o   Brown the mince in the pan and then add the vegetables and stock. Let it simmer until the potatoes are cooked. If the liquid hasn't thickened up, add the cornflour to a mug and mix with cold water until it has a toothpaste-like consistency. Add more water if needed. Then, gently add this to the pan and stir until completely dissolved. Keep stirring to thicken.
    - o   Mash the potatoes and add milk and butter.
    - o   Place everything on a plate and serve.

Chicken Breast Burgers and Home-made Chips- 1 hour. Serves 4.

- Ingredients
    - o   4 frozen chicken breasts, six medium potatoes, 4 table-spoons of oil (plus more for drizzling over chips), salt and pepper, lettuce, tomatoes, 1 onion and 4 buns (brioche works really well).
- Methods
    - o   Preheat the oven and place the chicken on a baking tray with the oil. Check the cooking instructions on the chicken for the required temperature (it's usually 180-200 degrees).

o   Peel and chop the potatoes into wedges. Place on another tray and drizzle with the oil. Add salt and pepper and place in oven on the shelf under the chicken.

o   While cooking, wash and chop the salad ready for the buns.

o   Turn the chicken and wedges at around 25 minutes.

o   When the meat and wedges are done, add the chicken to the buns along with the salad and serve with the wedges.

Useful websites

General

- National Curriculum - https://www.gov.uk/government/publications/national-curriculum-in-england-primary-curriculum

Admin

- http://studentteacher.weebly.com/pupil-tracker.html
- https://tips.uark.edu/using-blooms-taxonomy/
- https://www.tes.com/teaching-resource/outstanding-teacher-year-week-and-lesson-planner-organiser-11532330
- https://www.tes.com/teaching-resource/assessment-for-learning-afl-checking-tool-activate-10000948
- https://www.tes.com/teaching-resource/higher-order-question-cards-bloom-s-taxonomy-11516252
- https://www.tes.com/teaching-resource/plenary-selector-wheel-version-2-what-have-i-learnt-today-8-generic-plenary-activities-no-planning-11339688
- https://www.tes.com/teaching-resource/plenary-generator-plenary-wheel-students-shout-stop-to-choose-lesson-plenary-wheel-spins-11070152
- https://www.tes.com/teaching-resource/help-your-children-check-their-work-11526210
- https://www.tes.com/teaching-resource/marking-stickers-to-encourage-feedback-23-template-bundle-6378637
- https://cse.google.com/all **(for making custom search engines)**
- https://www.tes.com/teaching-resource/afl-powerpoints-6074613
- https://www.tes.com/teaching-resource/interactive-plenaries-for-afl-6074603
- http://theappliciousteacher.com/9-ways-engagement-lesson/
- https://www.atl.org.uk/advice-and-resources/tnqz/writing-reports
- http://m.twinkl.co.uk/

resource/t-c-7196-report-writing-bank-of-statements-all-subjects-year-1-to-6

- http://m.twinkl.co.uk/resource/t-t-2545688-teacher-planner
- http://m.twinkl.co.uk/resource/t-c-1566-5-minute-fillers-for-primary-nqts-ks2
- http://www.the-teacher-next-door.com/index.php/blog/63-blog-classroom-management/203-100-report-card-comments-you-can-use-now
- https://www.educatorstechnology.com/2013/05/top-101-ipad-apps-for-lesson-planning.html
- https://performingformonkeys.wordpress.com
- https://teachingbattleground.wordpress.com/2007/03/18/getting-terrored/
- https://community.tes.com/threads/what-makes-the-pgce-so-hard-for-everyone.412249/

Subscription Sites:

Literacy

- http://primarytools.co.uk/files/app%20on%20one%20sheet/Grammar%20and%20Punctuation%20Curriculum%20Draft%20on%20one%20sheet.pdf
- https://www.literacyshed.com
- https://cornerstoneseducation.co.uk/free-samples/
- http://m.twinkl.co.uk/resource/t2-e-3114-lks2-features-of-sentences-display-pack
  https://www.spag.com/

Mathematics

- https://www.tes.com/teaching-resources/shop/Miss-Becky
- http://www.mathematicshed.com/measuring-shed.html
- http://m.twinkl.co.uk/resource/t2-m-2337-ks2-maths-talk-sentence-starters-display-pack
- http://mathsticks.com/my/2016/02/the-maths-interview-lesson/
- http://nrich.maths.org/primary-upper

- https://sites.google.com/a/aetinet.org/aet-mathematics/home/page-number-2/curriculum-design
- http://www.math-salamanders.com/

Topic

- http://www.freetech4teachers.com/2017/01/the-climate-time-machine.html?m=1

Science

- https://imagido.co.uk/collections/life-cycles

PHSE

- http://m.twinkl.co.uk/resource/au-t-c-6836-100-circle-time-questions-to-ask-just-for-fun-cards

Miscellaneous

- http://m.twinkl.co.uk/resource/t-c-580-class-management-teacher-folder-complete-resource-pack
- http://m.twinkl.co.uk/resource/t-c-1493-primary-nqt-tips-and-checklist
- http://m.twinkl.co.uk/resource/t-c-786-ks1-classroom-set-up-pack-for-nqts
- http://m.twinkl.co.uk/resource/t-c-7196-report-writing-bank-of-statements-all-subjects-year-1-to-6
- http://m.twinkl.co.uk/resource/t-c-1200-behaviour-management-resource-pack
- http://m.twinkl.co.uk/resource/t-c-166-nqt-teaching-file-resource-pack
- http://m.twinkl.co.uk/resource/t c-750-new-curriculum-over-view-posters-year-1-to-6
- http://m.twinkl.co.uk/resource/t-c-1586-evidencing-nqt-standards
- http://m.twinkl.co.uk/resource/t-l-52300-lanyard-sized-blooms-taxonomy-questions-for-reading-cards
- http://www.twinkl.co.uk/blog/question-prompt-lanyard

Cover Several Topics

- https://www.teachingpacks.co.uk
- https://m.twinkl.co.uk (2014 curriculum - subject- tap on subject heading for key stage- year group)
- https://www.tes.com/teaching-resources/hub/primary
- http://www.supplybag.co.uk/emergency-lesson-plans/
- https://www.planbee.com/
- https://classroomsecrets.co.uk
- https://www.teachitprimary.co.uk (also has free resources)
- https://www.twinkl.co.uk/resources/planit-primary-teaching-resources/3
- https://www.saveteacherssundays.com
- http://www.goodstuffprimaryresources.com/

Free Sites:

Literacy

- http://www.pobble365.com
- http://www.bbc.co.uk/schools/teachers/ks2_lessonplans/english/
- http://www.bbc.co.uk/schools/websites/4_11/site/literacy.shtml
- http://www.talk4writing.co.uk/resources/
- https://blogsdothertsforlearningdotcodotuk.files.wordpress.com/2016/07/ks2-reading-question-stems.doc
- http://www.deepeningunderstanding.co.uk/

Mathematics

- http://www.bbc.co.uk/schools/teachers/ks2_lessonplans/maths/
- http://garyhall.org.uk/primary-maths-resources.php
- http://myminimaths.co.uk/
- https://thirdspacelearning.com/blog/primary-maths
- http://www.bbc.co.uk/schools/websites/4_11/site/numeracy.shtml

- http://garyhall.org.uk/maths-starters-ks2.html
- https://www.tes.com/teaching-resources/
  teaching-for-mastery-in-primary-maths/mathematicsmastery
- https://www.prodigygame.com/referral-c.php?utm_ex-
  pid=71678278-54.xPoVR4JxQi2jSMuh7EmIrw.2&utm_refer-
  rer=http%3A%2F%2Fm.facebook.com
- https://www.mathsisfun.com/index.htm
- http://whiterosemaths.com
- http://mathsticks.com/my/2016/02/
  the-maths-interview-lesson/
- http://www.kangaroomaths.com/kenny2.
  php?page=Kschemeks2
- http://www.kangaroomaths.com/free_resources/planning/
  st1to9_overview.pdf
- http://youvegotthismath.com/2015/12/21/fraction-of-the-
  day/ (good starter)
- http://www.transum.org
- https://www.tes.com/teaching-resource/
  pupil-assessment-afl-in-mathematics-6023482
- http://garyhall.org.uk/primary-maths-resources.php
- https://www.tes.com/news/school-news/breaking-views/
  how-plan-engaging-maths-lessons

Topic

- http://www.resourcd.com/@anthropologyexchange/file/index

History

- http://www.teachingideas.co.uk/history/contents.htm
- http://www.ancientcivilizations.co.uk/home_set.html
- http://www.learningcurve.gov.uk/
- http://www.tudorbritain.org/
- http://www.henrytudor.co.uk/
- http://www.headlinehistory.co.uk/

- http://www.primaryhistory.org/
- http://www.schoolslinks.co.uk/links_history.htm
- http://www.schoolhistory.co.uk/primaryindex.html
- http://www.qca.org.uk/history/innovating/
- http://www.bbc.co.uk/guides/z2dr4wx
- http://www.thinkinghistory.co.uk/index.php
- http://www.bbc.co.uk/schools/websites/4_11/site/history.shtml
- https://www.teachitprimary.co.uk/geography

Science

- http://www.bbc.co.uk/schools/teachers/ks2_lessonplans/science/
- http://www.naturegrid.org.uk/
- http://www.schoolingamonkey.com/rainbow-walking-water-science/
- http://www.bbc.co.uk/schools/scienceclips/index_flash.shtml
- http://www.exploratorium.edu/explore/handson.html
- http://www.globaleye.org.uk/primary_spring05/index.html
- http://www.primaryresources.co.uk/science/science.htm
- http://sciencelessons.digitalbrain.com/digitalbrain/web/subjects/1.%20primary/ks2sci/?verb=view
- http://www.nhm.ac.uk/nature-online//index.html
- https://www.tes.com/teaching-resource/teachers-tv-ks1-ks2-science-forces-6044061
- http://webarchive.nationalarchives.gov.uk/20100612050234/
- http://www.standards.dfes.gov.uk/schemes2/science/?view=get
- http://dragonsdencurriculum.blogspot.co.uk/2015/06/organisms-and-habitats_11.html?m=1
- http://www.bbc.co.uk/schools/websites/4_11/site/science.shtml

ICT

- http://www.kidsmart.org.uk/parents/

MFL

- http://www.rachelhawkes.com
- https://www.lightbulblanguages.co.uk
- http://www.lovelanguage.co.uk/store.html
- http://nattalingo.co.uk/spip.php?article148
- https://www.tes.com/teaching-resource/games-for-french-spanish-german-lessons-11526014?utm_campaign=RES-2073-20784108&utm_content=author-referral&utm_source=-facebook&utm_medium=social

PHSE

- http://www.bbc.co.uk/schools/websites/4_11/site/pshe.shtml
- https://www.tes.com/teaching-resource/assembly-about-friendship-for-ks1-and-ks2-primary-6051941
- https://www.tes.com/teaching-resource/british-values-11117639
- https://www.tes.com/teaching-resources/blog/best-reviewed-british-values-resources

RE

- http://www.cist.org.uk/pv/pm/pp1001.htm
- http://discoveryschemeofwork.com

PE

- https://primecoachingsport.wordpress.com/2016/12/15/60-awesome-pe-sport-station-activities-the-exploring-stations-pe-sport-skills-grades-k-3/

Miscellaneous

- http://www.parliament.uk/education/teaching-resources-lesson-plans/

- https://classroomsecrets.co.uk/ new-national-curriculum-objectives/
- https://hwb.gov.wales/Resources/ tree?sort=created&language=en
- https://teaching.uncc.edu/sites/teaching.uncc.edu/files/ media/files/file/GoalsAndObjectives/BloomWritingObjectives. pdf
- https://bouncyballs.org
- https://outstanding-lessons.wikispaces.com
- http://archive.teachfind.com/ttv/www.teachers.tv/series/ great-primary-lesson-ideas.html
- https://www.tes.com/articles/primary-lesson-plans

Phonics

- http://www.syntheticphonics.com/
- http://www.bbc.co.uk/schools/wordsandpictures/clusters/ index.shtml
- https://phonicbooks.wordpress.com/2011/12/01/ what-are-adjacent-consonants-3/
- http://www.lancsngfl.ac.uk/curriculum/literacy/lit_site/ lit_sites/phonemes_001/
- http://moortown.leeds.sch.uk/wp-content/uploads/2013/01/ Phonics-and-Graphemes.pdf
- http://www.enchantedlearning.com/consonantblends/
- http://www.kizphonics.com/what-is-phonics/
- http://www.theschoolrun.com/what-magic-e

Cover Several Topics

- http://studentteacher.weebly.com
- http://www.primaryideas.co.uk/
- http://www.free-teaching-resources.co.uk/lesson-ideas/ maths/maths-ks1/index.html
- http://www.primaryresources.co.uk/
- http://www.ks2complete.com

Blogs

- https://primarymusings.wordpress.com
- https://lovetoteach87.wordpress.com
- https://nataliehscott.wordpress.com
- http://www.teachingandlearningguru.com
- http://hecticteacher.com/blog
- https://mrshumanities.com
- http://bex-trex2teaching.blogspot.co.uk/?m=1
- http://ebbucation.blogspot.co.uk/?m=1
- http://iteachpsych.tumblr.com/post/138675554284/ behaviour-techniques

University To-Do List

Both a blank and example version can be found on the website:

https://survivingyourpgce.com/category/resources/

Printed in Great Britain
by Amazon

61891650R00088